HITLER

A. N. WILSON

HITLER

BASIC BOOKS

A Member of the Perseus Books Group
New York

Published by Basic Books,
A Member of the Perseus Books Group
387 Park Avenue South
New York, NY 10016

Books published by Basic Books are available at special discounts for bulk purchases
in the United States by corporations, institutions, and other organizations. For more
information, please contact the Special Markets Department at the Perseus Books
Group, 2300 Chestnut Street, Suite 200, Philadelphia, PA 19103, or call (800) 810-4145,
ext. 5000, or e-mail special.markets@perseusbooks.com.

Cataloging-in-Publication data for the hardcover edition are available from the
Library of Congress.

ISBN (hardcover): 978-0-465-03128-3
ISBN (e-book): 978-0-465-03137-5

10 9 8 7 6 5 4 3 2 1

To Ruth, with love.

CONTENTS

ONE

'In that Hour it Began'

As the German Chancellor, Hitler instigated the mass-murder of as many as 6 million Jews. He forced Western Europe, and eventually the whole world, into a calamitous war in which over 50 million Europeans were killed. When he committed suicide in 1945, he left his country a burning heap of ruins, financially bankrupt, militarily abject, physically wrecked. It is not surprising, then, that his reputation in history is demonic. Even though Mao Tse-tung and Stalin killed more people, and history since 1945 has thrown up such monsters as Pol Pot, Hitler has retained his place as the Demon King of history, the ultimate horror-tyrant. For this reason alone, we feel compelled to revisit the story of his life. In so doing, we perhaps want to pretend that his repellent life-views, which drove him to his acts of mayhem and murder, were somehow unique to himself, or if not quite unique, then at least special to the Nazi movement he led. To some degree – if we are thinking of the crazier theories relating to blood purity, or the quasi-religious cult of violence based on a return to the

1

mythologies of the pagan north – then we should be right to think that Hitler had nothing in common with the decent bourgeois majority of Europeans of his generation. He was a freak, a satanic oddity, a demon.

But this picture of him is not completely tenable. In general, Hitler embodied the views of any popular newspaper, any bar-parlour bore, from England to Russia, from Finland to Sicily, during his lifetime: that is, that science had replaced religion; that Darwin had mysteriously 'explained' everything about the struggles of history, that the fittest would survive, and that among the differing peoples of the earth, it was the 'Aryan' or Eurasian race who were superior to the 'savages' found in Africa and South America, or to the Jews. His view, ranted aloud through microphones to rallies of thousands, that the Jews were both the sinister powers at work behind the banks and the stock markets, contriving the world's ruin, and at the same time they were the 'disease' eating away at your savings with anti-capitalist, Bolshevist plots, was a fear which did not vanish even when his whole regime had been ground to rubble by his enemies.

A spectre was haunting Europe. It was not Communism, as Marx and Engels had proclaimed in 1848, though Communism was a part of the spectre. It was bankruptcy. And that spectre had haunted Europe ever since the prodigy of modern industrial capitalism began in England in the eighteenth century. When things went well, the system produced comfort and leisure of a kind unimagined by the human race at any previous period of history. But there always existed, like some curse in a fairy tale, the possibility that things would go wrong, and that the safe comfortable world created by capitalism could, through no fault of the families or individuals concerned, plunge the working classes into starvation and the middle classes into the disgrace of debt and penury. The prosperous *parfumeur* César Birotteau in Balzac's novel of that name suddenly becomes an abject pauper. He did not realize that in expanding his business he was taking on debts with a scurrilous banker. Like so many of the characters in Balzac's great *Human Comedy*, that series of books which defined the nineteenth century to itself much more vividly than did Karl Marx, Birotteau is one minute prosperous, and the next up to his neck in debt. That swoop, from prosperity to absolute degradation, is the single greatest dread among the middle classes created by nineteenth-century capitalism. You see it in the novels of Dickens and Balzac over and over again. You see it in the genre paintings, of a middle-class family having to sell up their last belongings. Whether you are upper middle class, like the Sedleys in Thackeray's *Vanity Fair*, or lower middle class like Adolf Hitler, the spectre is haunting you all the time. Something might happen in the world's stock markets which suddenly ruins you.

'Old John Sedley was ruined' ... and Thackeray shows us all his belongings being picked over and sold off at auction. 'The Hebrew aide de camp in the service of the officer at the table bid against the Hebrew gentleman employed by the elephant purchasers and a brisk battle ensued over this little piano.'[1] Part of the mythos of capitalism was that mysteriously it was controlled and exploited by the Jews. When there is a lurch in the stock market or when there is a run on the banks, the Jews will somehow emerge from the crisis unscathed – having made their profit out of your misfortune.

The basic self-contradiction of the anti-Semitic conspiracy theory – that Jews control both the capitalist system and the Communism which sought to overthrow it – did not die with Nazism. It resurfaces even now, either implicitly or explicitly, in journalism and commentary in any country in the world. Hitler's anti-Semitism was a mania of advanced degree but it was very far from being unusual, and although few like to admit it, his hatred of the Jews was one important element in his easy rise to power. Hitler and the Nazis expressed themselves with a crudity you may not think would have gone down well in, say, a London publishing house. Yet his prejudice was one shared with the poetry editor of Faber and Faber, T. S. Eliot – 'The Jew is underneath the lot.'

Adolf Hitler – remarkably, in a man whose father was the son of an illegitimate housemaid – had grown up with the middle-class confidence that he need never earn a living. When he first emerged so astonishingly onto the European stage, he might have appeared provincial and uncouth. But he belonged to a class which had savings. He belonged to the shabby-genteel class, the class which perhaps more than any other feels the shame of social descent through poverty. Aspirant members of this class, throughout Europe and America, have traditionally struggled to 'better' themselves, fearing idleness, bohemianism, any of the eccentricities or cultivations which might lead grander social classes to an amusing decadence, but which lead the petits bourgeois back to the working classes from which they struggled.

Had his father, a customs official in various border towns between Austria-Hungary and Germany, lived to see the publication of Hitler's autobiography, *Mein Kampf* (*My Struggle*), he might well have asked, 'What Struggle?' Alois Hitler had indeed known struggle, and so had his third wife, Hitler's mother, Klara Pölzl. Alois, whose early life had marked a real struggle to leave poverty behind, and to acquire respectability and savings through boring government service in customs offices, had urged young Adolf to find paid employment. The boy had preferred to lounge about, to wear dandified clothes, to attend the opera and to imagine that one day he would become a famous artist, or maybe a composer of operas, like his hero Richard Wagner. When his father died in 1903, and his mother followed him to the grave four years later, Hitler had never in his life looked for paid work. He had assumed that he would be able to live on savings. He would study at the Academy of Fine Arts in Vienna, and maybe become a great architectural artist, perhaps an architect who would rebuild Linz, the provincial city where he had attended the Realschule and not done especially well. A fellow pupil was another oddball, Ludwig Wittgenstein, but there is no evidence that they even spoke to one another at school. Wittgenstein was not noted, at any period of life, for his easy manners, and Hitler, until he had completed military service, appears to have been paralysed with shyness and silence in most circumstances.

Wittgenstein at different times of his life had paid work – as a village schoolmaster, as a lab assistant in a London hospital, and as a don at Cambridge. Hitler never had any paid employment, so far as one can make out, except when manual work was forced upon him as a temporary necessity when he was living in men's hostels and dosshouses on the outskirts of Vienna. In fact, he had not done well enough at school to get a good job. He failed to get into the Academy of Fine Arts in Vienna and gradually slithered downhill from the position of comfort and prosperity into which he had been born to one of penniless indigence. He lived among the homeless in men's hostels, tried to sell his (usually postcard-size) architectural paintings. When this was happening, Europe was not going through a phase of unemployment, such as plagued the 1920s and 1930s. He could have taken a job as a waiter or a clerk or done something in exchange for pay, the way that almost everyone in the world is expected to do. Never once did he do so. Nor, as far as history throws any light on the matter, did he ever consider it necessary to pay his own way. The flats he lived in when he became successful, the cars he drove, the clothes he wore were all supplied by other people. Even his beloved dogs, Prinz, Muckl, Wolf and Blondi, were gifts. He was a domestic incompetent. When his niece killed herself he needed to import housemaids immediately into his Munich apartment.

Hitler's indolence was to remain one of his most mysterious characteristics. Many would assume that a man who, in his heyday, strutted about in uniforms, and who presided over a militaristic dictatorship, who expected not merely his

intimates but everyone in the country to click their heels and
salute at the mere mention of his name, would have been up
in the morning early, taking cold baths and performing
Swedish exercises. By contrast, like many depressives, he kept
strange hours, and spent most of his days on this planet
sitting around doing nothing much, dreaming his terrible
dreams, and talking interminable nonsense. In this he was
extraordinarily unlike the archetypical Germans who looked
to him in the 1920s and 1930s as their saviour. They were
hard-working, home-loving people who, by the end of the
1920s, had received two catastrophic buffets from fate. The
first was their country's defeat in the First World War, and the
second – a direct consequence of the first calamity – was
financial ruin. Hitler's own 'struggle' had in fact been entirely
of his own making, and was due to simple laziness. There had
been nothing to stop him, as a young man, giving up his
unrealistic plans to become an artist and taking a job in an
office. But he could not bring himself to get out of bed in the
mornings. Hence his own slide into poverty. But he made his
ruin into a personal myth with which a whole bankrupted
nation was able to identify. All those hard-worked clerks and
small businessmen and waiters and factory workers who
voted for Hitler – while they were still allowed to vote – and
who saw him as their national saviour, were quite, quite
different from Hitler. Their ruin had not been as a result of
idleness, or dreaminess. It had been caused by their militaristic Kaiser and his right-wing government leading them into
a disastrous and costly war. For this war, the German people

were made, by international treaty, quite literally to pay. Whenever there was a chance of economic recovery in the 1920s, Germany had to face the reparations demanded by France. Had the Germans been able to mine the coal in the Ruhr or exploit the great steelworks of that industrial region, there would have been some chance of a post-war economic recovery. But this industrial heartland had been occupied by the French in 1923. So in this impossible situation, the German people found themselves seduced by a political movement which appeared to offer them a solution, led by a man whose own life-journey, as set to the weird opera which must have played itself continually inside his head, matched their own national crisis.

Many books not written in German playfully use the German word for Leader – *Führer* – to refer to him. It has become a sort of nickname: the Führer. But although the Leader appeared quite literally as a saviour to the unemployed Germans whom he restored to labour, to the homeowners and rentiers whose lifetime investments he appeared to make safe, he was far from being a typical German. He was indeed not a German at all and only received German citizenship in 1932, shortly before becoming Chancellor. The fact that he found himself in Munich in May 1913, as an indigent, penniless artist and layabout, was owing to the fact that he was a draft dodger from the Austro-Hungarian army.

From 1910 – when Hitler was twenty to twenty-one – the Austrian authorities had been pursuing him to do his national service in the Imperial army. When they came after him, he denied that he had left Vienna to avoid the army. It was poverty, he claimed, which prevented him from coming to Salzburg in order to plead ill health. After a long exchange of letters he did eventually go to Salzburg, a comparatively short journey by train from Munich, and submit to a medical examination, and it was agreed that the underfed, gloomy young man was too weak to bear arms and should be pronounced unfit for military service.

And herein lies the peculiar mystery of the Hitler phenomenon. Hitler was almost without any skills at all. He had very little energy, a modest education, no obvious 'leadership' qualities, and in many respects almost no interest in politics. In party politics he had no interest whatsoever. Nor, when in power, was he a 'micromanager'. He was a peculiar combination of absolute controller and idler. There was scarcely any area of government business or military organization over which he did not wish to exercise personal control; but the day-to-day business either of civil or military administration was often something to which he appeared to demonstrate airy indifference. The tantrum was used as a workable substitute for practical common sense. Presumably he had known since childhood that most people will do anything to avoid a scene, so that a willingness to make scenes, explosive scenes, over the most trivial of upsets, or for no observable reason at all, would give him power over almost anyone with whom he came into contact – party apparatchiks, generals, foreign heads of state.

For twelve years, this man who had no obvious talent for anything except public speaking, the manipulation of crowds, and the manipulation of individuals through emotional bullying, dominated European history. For the first six of those years, he performed what appeared to be an economic miracle: he led his country out of the gravest economic crisis ever to face a developed economy in the Western world, and he gave it full employment and apparent prosperity. He then proceeded to invade, annex or conquer Austria, the greater part of Czechoslovakia and the disputed German lands which had been appropriated by the French. All this was accomplished with astonishingly little loss of life. No wonder he was regarded, in the period 1933–9, as a hero. The British Prime Minister who had presided over victory in the First World War, the Liberal leader David Lloyd George, was overwhelmed when he visited Hitler's Germany in 1936. Lloyd George's daughter mockingly exclaimed 'Heil Hitler!' 'Certainly Heil Hitler!' replied Lloyd George in all seriousness, 'I say it because he is a really great man.' On his return to England, Lloyd George wrote an article for Lord Beaverbrook's *Daily Express* (then a newspaper which was taken seriously), describing Hitler as a born leader of men, trusted by the old, idolized by the young, who had lifted his country from the depths.

Anyone meeting Hitler twenty years before, however, and staring into the face of that pale, lonely youth, would have agreed that he was not fit either for military life or for anything else of a very practical bent. His Munich landlady in 1913–14, Frau Popp, a tailor's wife, afterwards described her lodger as quiet, who spent much of his time painting his postcards – characterless little architectural studies which leave no impression at all. He was also, she remembered, a voracious reader. She does not tell us what he was reading. Hitler's later conversation suggests retentive, rather than wide, reading. He could quote whole pages of the gloomy philosopher Schopenhauer, who had been of such profound influence over Hitler's hero, Richard Wagner. He probably read Wagner's libretti as poetry. He read *Uncle Tom's Cabin*, *Gulliver's Travels* and *Don Quixote*. His favourite author, however, was Karl May. Even as Reich Chancellor Hitler would still be urging his generals to try May's novels – upbraiding them for their lack of imagination when they failed to see the point of them. May is not a popular author in the English-speaking world but he still has his following in Germany. He modelled himself on Fenimore Cooper and his best-known stories are set among the American Indians. The American Indian Winnetou and the cowboy Surehand are the best known of his heroes. As a devoted pacifist, May was in many ways a surprising choice of literary hero for a future war leader. His stories, both those set in the American West and those which deal with the Near East, such as *In the Land of the Mahdi* and *From Baghdad to Istambul*, are stories set in exotic landscapes in which heroes battle against impossible odds and triumph through an exercise of the will.

Hitler's childhood and family background have been endlessly studied for clues which would explain his later development. At the beginning of *My Struggle*, he himself emphasized the geographical importance of having been born in Braunau am Inn, a town in a provincial part of the Austro-Hungarian Empire. Writing in 1923–4, he saw the unification of the two great German states as desirable. 'German-Austria must once more be reunited with the great German Motherland: and not just for economic reasons. No, no! Even if reunification had no economic advantages one way or another, even if it were positively disadvantageous, it must still take place. *One Blood belongs together in One Reich.*'[2] It was one of the fundamental planks of his foreign policy, and it could clearly be seen with hindsight that the expansionism which lay behind this idea would lead inevitably to the European war which followed in the year after the Anschluss (literally, the 'Connexion'; it is the word used for the annexation of Austria by Germany).

We see, from the very first page of *My Struggle*, how Hitler made his own childhood part of the whole political German story. It was Fate (*Schicksal*) which determined where he was born. And the fact that he was the son of a customs officer, an official who by definition stood at the border, was made to have mystic significance.

His father had been born Alois Schicklgruber in 1837. He had risen from the peasantry. Much has been made of Alois's violence. Most fathers in history have beaten their children, not a few have had fiery tempers. None has had a son like Adolf Hitler. Alois Schicklgruber was the illegitimate son of a woman named Maria Anna Schicklgruber. All sorts of fantasies have been spun about the possible father, including the untenable view that he might have been Jewish. Five years after Alois was born, his mother married a fifty-year-old miller's journeyman named Johann Georg Hiedler. His mother died when he was five, and Alois was then taken to live on Johann Georg's brother's farm. The brother was Johann Nepomuk, the grandfather of Hitler's mother, Klara. (Hence her calling Alois 'uncle' when she married him.) Alois worked hard and rose in status. By 1876, he had managed to persuade a notary in Weitra that he should be legitimized. The overwhelming likelihood is that his father was in fact Johann Georg Hiedler and in the legitimization papers, this name is spelt Hitler. Thus the name entered history. Hiedler/Hüttler/Hitler all are variations of the same name, which means a smallholder or one who lives in a hut. Either way, Fate/*Schicksal* was kind to the future Adolf in giving him a snappy two-syllabled name. Somehow the great Nuremberg rallies would not have seemed so impressive if the serried ranks of tens of thousands of enthusiastic Germans had all been chanting 'Heil Schicklgruber!'

Alois's first marriage was childless. His second produced a son, also called Alois, who married an Irish girl called Bridget Dowling, who lived for a while in Liverpool, England, and whose child, William Patrick Hitler, was born in 1911 and later lived in New York. The other child was Angela, who for a while kept house for Adolf Hitler, and whose daughter by Leo Raubal – also called Angela (Geli) – was Hitler's beloved niece.

It was as his third wife that Alois Hitler took Klara Pölzl. There were five children – Gustav, who died aged two in 1887;

Ida who also died in infancy; Otto who died as a baby; Edmund who died aged sixteen in 1900, Paula who lived until 1960 and Adolf, who was born on 20 April 1889.

Given the high mortality rate of his siblings, and the fact that both parents were dead by the time he was eighteen, it was not surprising that Hitler was a hypochondriac who always feared illness and imagined his own life would be a short one.

By the time he was living with his widowed mother, the family had settled in the somewhat dingy provincial town of Linz. There was real tension in the town between the German nationalist population – numbering about 60,000 – and the Czechs. Alois Hitler was a passionate German nationalist. Adolf absorbed and inherited these feelings: they may be said to have determined his entire foreign policy, and all the expansionism of 1936–9 which brought the world to the war. What he did not inherit, as has already been said, was any of his father's desire to work hard and better himself.

He was a moody, idle, and not especially talented child. When Alois died in 1903, he left the family reasonably comfortable. The three women of the family – mother Klara, aunt Johanna and little sister Paula – did all the work of running the apartment. His mother bought Adolf a grand piano and for four months he took lessons. He was a competent pianist, and had a good ear. He was a lonely, withdrawn boy. His only known emotional excitement was having a painful crush on a girl called Stefanie, a beautiful young lady he saw in the streets of Linz. There is no evidence that they even so much as spoke to one another. His best friend was a musician named August Kubizek – Gustl. It was he who told us, in his largely adulatory memoir of his friendship with Hitler, of his friend's life in those days. It was with Gustl that Hitler first sampled the opera – Hitler clad on these occasions in a black coat and opera hat, and carrying a cane with an ivory handle. It was with Gustl that Hitler, aged twelve, first attended *Lohengrin*. On one evening the two friends saw a production of Wagner's *Rienzi*, an early opera (more like Weber musically than it is like the later, developed Wagner). The opera tells the story of a young demagogue in fourteenth-century Rome who led his people to rebellion, and was finally rejected by them. Doubts have been cast by historians upon Kubizek's recollection of this evening in which, after the performance, Hitler is supposed to have climbed the Freinberg, the mountain outside Linz, and been in a sort of prophetic trance. As Kubizek reconstructed the scene in 1939 for Winifred Wagner at the Bayreuth Opera House, Hitler is supposed to have added, mysteriously, 'In that hour it began.'

In jener Stunde begann es.

In fact what happened to Hitler in the next few years was about as far from any Rienzi-like political awakening as it is possible to imagine. He and Kubizek went to Vienna and shared a flat together. Kubizek studied music at the Conservatoire. Hitler was supposed to be at the Academy of Fine Arts, but had in fact failed the entry exams twice.

It has been plausibly conjectured that Hitler broke with his friend because he could not stand the shame of this failure.

Hitler's mother died of breast cancer in 1907. The doctor attending her said that he had never seen anyone so prostrate with grief as was Hitler when his mother died. Eduard Bloch, the doctor, was Jewish, and neither Hitler nor his sister seem to have felt, or demonstrated, any anti-Semitic feeling towards him, still less blamed him for Klara's death. The anti-Semitic mania appears to have developed later, perhaps during Hitler's mysterious years as a drop-out student in Vienna.

For he soon got through the money his mother had left him, and he never appears to have taken employment. Some more money was due to him from his father's will when he reached – on 20 April 1913 – the age of twenty-four. Much of his time was spent simply waiting in idleness for this date to arrive. In May 1913, wanted by the Austrian police because he had failed to register for military service, he escaped over the German border and went to live in Munich.

There then occurred the event which, as Ian Kershaw, the great British Hitler scholar, has said 'made Hitler possible':[3] the outbreak of the First World War. Having persuaded the Austrian authorities that he was medically unfit for service, he had returned to Munich. But, like so very many young men in 1914, Hitler was caught up in war fever when the great European powers – Russia, Austro-Hungary, Germany and Britain, together with France – found themselves edging towards war after the heir to the Austro-Hungarian Empire, the Archduke Franz Ferdinand, was assassinated by a young Serbian terrorist in Sarajevo. Although serious politicians and diplomats saw the outbreak of war as a calamity, and the more far-sighted were able to see that it could destroy Western civilization, the public mood was buoyant. With the declaration of hostilities, there were happy, cheering crowds in all the major cities of Europe. In one of these cheering crowds, in the Odeonsplatz in Munich, a camera by extraordinary chance captured the young, exultant face of Adolf Hitler, a nonentity unknown to anyone, just as he was about to enlist with the Bavarian army. Although in 1870, with the creation of the German nation under Bismarck's Prussia, it had come into political union, Bavaria was traditionally separate from the rest of Germany until 1918. Hitler had to write a personal application to old King Ludwig III to join his army. He was turned down by the first regiment to which he applied – the Bavarian King's Own – but he was accepted by the 1st Bavarian Infantry Regiment.

It used to be believed by historians that Hitler was, if not a war hero, then at least a conspicuously brave front-line soldier. New research by Dr Thomas Weber of Aberdeen University has uncovered a confusion about what was meant by a regimental runner, which was Hitler's job in the army. Battalion or company runners did indeed have a dangerous job, running between different trenches in the front line of battle under heavy machine-gun fire. Hitler, however, was something rather different – a regimental runner. The regimental runners worked several miles from the front in regimental headquarters. They were office boys in military uniform. One man who did the same job, Alois Schnelldorfer, wrote to his parents that his job was no more dangerous than to sit in an armchair and make calls to their postmistress. 'I can drink a litre of beer and sit down under a walnut tree', he wrote home.

The men among whom Hitler served considered him a strange bird. They noted his teetotalism, and his aloofness from their jokes and conversation. He would sit apart from them, reading history (perhaps in fact Karl May novels?), writing letters (to his mother-substitute, the Munich land-lady Frau Popp) and sketching. They nicknamed him 'the artist' or 'the painter'. They mocked his physical incompetence. He could not open cans of meat with a bayonet as they all could, and they ribbed him that if he worked in a canning factory he would starve to death.[4]

One thing they noticed was his slavishness to superiors. And it paid off. Dr Weber's new research has shown that it was comparatively easy for an infantryman to win an Iron Cross, First Class, if he was in constant touch with the officers. Hitler was lucky enough to be recommended for this honour by Hugo Gutmann, a Jewish adjutant, who, in 1937, was to be put in prison by the Gestapo. Luckily for Gutmann, his old comrades in the regiment petitioned for his release and he was able to escape to the United States, but not thanks to Hitler. The best friend he made in the army was a white terrier dog who had escaped from an English trench. Hitler called him 'little Fox' or Fuchsl. 'With exemplary patience (he did not understand a word of German) I got him used to me,' he wrote back to Frau Popp in Munich.

It is not surprising, therefore, given Hitler's comparatively safe job well behind enemy lines, that he was able to survive so well on the Western Front, in spite of his regiment taking part in some of the worst battles of the war, such as the Somme in 1916 in which over 600,000 young men were killed. It is also revealing that when he did suffer injury, it was not because he was running on an errand, but sitting in a tunnel close to regimental HQ when a shell hit the roof. Hitler's plea to his Lieutenant, Wiedemann, when he was put on a stretcher, 'But I can still stay with you? Stay with the regiment? Can't I?', has often been taken as evidence that he was still anxious, even in his injuries, to be fighting for the Fatherland; but it could just as well be seen as a sign that for the first time in his life, in the regiment, and surrounded by men in uniform, he had found an environment in which he felt comfortable and at home. This is not to say that he was homosexual. Very many lonely men, or men whose lives had been humdrum or unsatisfactory in civilian life, felt the same, during both world wars, when they enlisted in the services.

He was invalided out of the regiment and was taken first to a field hospital, then to a military hospital just south of Berlin before being transferred to a replacement battalion in Munich. It is here that we begin to see the signs of that virulent anti-Semitism which in the next few years became a trademark mania. He noticed that all the clerks were Jews, and began to hatch the view that the Jews had somehow sapped national morale, or were responsible for the failure of the German army to make headway on the Western Front.

He was eventually allowed to return to his old regiment in the line, and there was a glad reunion with little Fuchsl, who was by now in Ypres, Belgium. The first night they were together, Hitler took Fuchsl ratting and stabbed many a rat with his bayonet. The regiment took part in the Third Battle of Ypres, but for the rest of 1917 saw no action. There was plenty more time for playing with the dog and reading Karl May novels. In Russia, the Bolshevik Revolution took place, and throughout all the armies of Europe – German, French and British – the spectre of Communism began to haunt the officer classes.

In 1918, the regiment was ordered back to Flanders. In March the men heard that the German Government had made peace with the Soviet Government of Russia at Brest-Litovsk. Early in September 1918 the regiment was again moved back to Flanders, but Hitler had a period of leave and with a comrade named Arendt he spent it in Berlin, where the mood of revolution was palpable.

Hitler returned to his regiment for what was to be the last month of the war. It was in the area below Ypres that they dug into the fields and hills near Comines. Near the village of Wervick, on 14 October, there was a gas attack. Hitler felt scalding in his eyes, and was taken off, temporarily blinded, to hospital at Pasewalk in Pomerania. He had survived the war. At the Nuremberg trials, following the Second World War, the adjutant of the regiment gave evidence. He said that there had sometimes arisen a question of promoting Hitler from the ranks and making him a non-commissioned officer. Whenever the matter was discussed, however, it was always decided in the negative, 'because we could discover no leadership qualities in him'. Furthermore, Otfrid Förster, a renowned neuro-surgeon who saw Hitler's medical file in 1932, gave it as his opinion that Hitler's blindness was a case of 'hysterical ambly-opia'.[5] If this were the case, and it seems highly likely, then we can discount the gas attack altogether and lose the last shred of a claim that Hitler the messenger boy had an 'heroic' war.

In *My Struggle*, needless to say, the end of the war, and Hitler's part in it, had to be given a quality of apocalypse. On 10 November, the hospital chaplain brought the patients news that a revolution had broken out in Berlin and that the Imperial Royal House, the Hohenzollerns, had gone into exile in Holland. The Kaiser was no more. Germany was a socialist republic. The revolution had been achieved by 'a few Jewish youths ... who had not been at the Front'.[6]

Saint Paul, although in Hitler's eyes a dangerous Jewish Bolshevik, had been struck blind by God before going into Damascus and beginning his great mission to convert the world. It would seem that a comparable miracle was performed by Providence upon Adolf Hitler. When the chaplain broke the news of Germany's defeat, it was sad, naturally, for all Germans. But for the author of *My Struggle*, this was a personal thing. 'While everything became black before my eyes, I teetered and groped my way back towards the ward, threw myself on my bunk, and buried my burning head into my blanket and pillow. I had not shed a tear since the day that I stood beside my mother's grave. When, in my youth, Fate grabbed me with-out mercy, my defiant resolve only quickened. When in the long years of war, death took so many comrades and friends from among our ranks, it would have seemed a sin to me to bewail their fate – they died for Germany!'[7]

He bore all these sorrows. He endured blindness and pain without a murmur, it would seem. But what drew forth his tears was the left-wing revolution. For ever afterwards, the 'November criminals', the socialists who concluded the Armistice on 11 November 1918, were the villains of the story which Hitler told – first to himself, then to his small gang of political cronies, then to larger groups, and finally to Germany and to the world. *My Struggle* asks us to believe that it was while he lay weeping on his hospital bed that he decided to go into politics. Whether or not such a decision was made, there would have been no hope, in the old world, that a man of Hitler's background, with no obvious qualifications, could enter the political sphere. But the world had changed. With the coming of the peace, the world was ready for the arrival of this dreamer. Unheeding, Germany moved into the humiliations, poverty and chaos of its post-war life. It was to be some years before Germany woke up to the fact that its Lohengrin had arrived, though not by swan; that its Rienzi had arisen, though not from Rome. When he was discharged from hospital, with his sight fully recovered, and ordered to report to the replacement battalion of his old regiment, he was the reverse of 'demob happy', since it was by no means clear what possible avocation in civilian life this failed art student who had never done a job might follow. As for his little friend, Fuchsl, history does not relate what happened to him, but he presumably ended his war in Belgium.

TWO

'Our Leader'

When Hitler left the army he had no prospects, no money, no professional skill, no social contacts. Yet within a mere fourteen years he would become Chancellor of the German Reich, a man before whom generals and admirals sycophantically cringed, before whom foreign heads of state bowed, a hero of the masses who had become not so much a popular hero as a divinity on the pattern of the old Roman emperors. We will come nowhere close to understanding this mystery if we attempt to endow Hitler with too many qualities, either of good or of evil. He rose fast because he had so little weight to carry. He had been an obedient soldier – though his commanding officers believed he possessed no leadership qualities, and history, broadly speaking, proved them right unless you believe that such qualities include the ability to lead vast masses to total disaster. He had a good ear and with the skill of a good conductor he could pick out the different instrument parts in an orchestra. But he was only an averagely good pianist. He had aspirations to be a great artist or architect but his drawings were pedestrian. He had no competence in foreign tongues. He made clever use of his reading but that reading was extremely limited. Indeed, it was the very fact of his limitations which gave him such strength. He had few abilities and it was these which carried him along.

Chief and greatest of his gifts was the capacity to speak in public, a gift which had lain dormant throughout his tongue-tied youth. The gift first manifested itself when he was a young soldier, on the verge of demobilization in 1919, and was quickly seized on by his commanding officers and used to combat Communism among the troops. Germany had been declared a republic. The Kaiser, the grandson of Queen Victoria, had gone into exile in Holland – one of his first requests being for a 'good strong cup of English tea'. The Social Democrat Republican Government in Berlin was left with the ignominious task of agreeing the peace on the victors' terms. The German army had never been defeated in any major land battle throughout the war. In the end, the entry of the Americans into the European war at a very late stage, with their huge resources of men and weapons, simply exhausted the German leadership, and the generals, including General Erich Ludendorff (who would emerge as the natural political leader of the post-war German Right), agreed to the surrender. But the Right never acknowledged this messy circumstance. Immediately they invented the myth that the 'November criminals', the Social Democrats, egged on by Communists and Jews, had drawn Germany into a humiliation from which radical right-wing despotism could alone save it.

In Berlin, the Republican government was perpetually threatened, on the one hand by the furious voices of the Right (who ranged from old royalists who were shocked by the emperor's abdication, to those who would favour a military dictatorship) and by the enormous power and influence of the Communists. In Bavaria, where the Wittelsbach Dynasty abandoned its crown, the Communists did actually for a short while take over until they were replaced by a right-wing republic led by Gustav von Kahr. The Treaty of Brest-Litovsk had been signed a few months before Germany capitulated to France, Britain and America. In this treaty, the Russians signed away large tracts of land which would the following year be given back to them by the terms of the Treaty of Versailles. The Communist government of Lenin had every reason to hope that the discontented soldiers of the German army and the hard-pressed German working classes, suffering enormous post-war hardship, would turn to Communism.

It was this which the German officer class was determined to resist. Seventy miles to the west of Munich was the camp of Lechfeld where thousands of troops, returning prisoners of war and others, were assembled before being discharged into civilian life. The camp was 'Bolshevistically and Spartacistically contaminated' – according to the officer in charge. (Spartacist was another word for the Communist movement after the leader of the Roman slave rebels, Spartacus.) Hitler was among those soldiers enlisted into the 'education detachment', the Aufklärungskommando, to speak to these would-be Communists and persuade them of the dangers of the Red Peril. This was in July 1919, when the Treaty of Versailles, with all its unfairness, was a source of agony to all Germans. Hitler denounced the Treaty, he denounced the Communists and he denounced the international capitalist financiers and Jews whom he held responsible for having started the war in the first instance.

There could be no doubt that Hitler had the gift of the gab. 'Herr Hitler, if I may put it this way, is the born people's orator', wrote an approving member of this early audience, 'and by his fanaticism and his crowd appeal he clearly compels the attention of his listeners, and makes them think his way.'[1]

Together with his actual ability to manipulate an audience, Hitler also showed an intuitive sense which amounted to genius that the spoken word was going to be of more significance than the written word in the coming years. Even the Communists, with their belief in harnessing the power of the often illiterate masses, clung to a belief in the written text which showed them to be the natural heirs of Gutenberg, Luther and Caxton. From the beginnings of Communism in the early nineteenth century to its crisis or unravelling in the 1970s, Communism remained, among other things, a doctrine, whose texts, like the Koran or the Talmud, could be endlessly re-perused by the Doctors of the Church, and interpreted in a literary way. They belonged to the vanishing world of the text; Hitler belonged to the oral future, the future which contained Walt Disney, television and cinema.

'The greatest revolutions in this world have never been directed by a pen! [The irony appears heavier in German, because the word for pen is feather.] No, the only thing the pen has been able to do is to provide theoretical foundations. But the power which has always set rolling the greatest religious and political avalanches in history from time immemorial has been the magic power [*die Zauberkraft*] of the spoken word.'[2]

Zauberkraft. From the beginning he saw himself as a magician. In fact, his sense of the power of the spoken word, the word blared through a loud-hailer, the word broadcast on radio and in film, was very far from being some ancient truth which had rolled down the ages from time immemorial. It was completely modern as in most respects he was. You can not imagine Hitler emerging as an eminent figure in any century before the twentieth. To this degree alone he is the supreme 'eminent life' of the twentieth century because in many respects he embodies it. He foreshadows Hollywood and television stars, and all the post-war politicians, of the free world as well as of the dictatorships, who depended for their success on their ability to present themselves on screen – a consideration which would have probably ditched the careers of most true political orators or administrative geniuses, from Pericles to Churchill (who was hopeless at TV). 'The destiny of Peoples can only be changed by a storm of hot passion and only he who carries such passion within himself can arouse it in others. Such passion alone gives its Chosen One the words which like hammer blows can open the gates to the heart of a people. But the man whose passion fails and whose lips are sealed – he has not been chosen by heaven to proclaim its will. Therefore, let the writer remain by his ink-well …'[3]

Hitler, together with Pathé, the pioneer of cinematic news-reels, and together with the Hollywood producers and the early pioneers of sound broadcasting, saw that the twentieth century was going to leave behind the printed word. Germany had invented printing. Under Hitler's dictatorship, Germany would burn its books. Gutenberg's printing press created a revolution in human consciousness. It created a freedom which no Inquisition or procurator could entirely suppress. With the widespread distribution of printed matter, anyone capable of reading could study, and re-read texts and make up their own minds.

Hitler was the first and the most hypnotic artist of post-literacy.

And so it was, in that frenzied atmosphere of post-war German army camps, that Hitler had his first taste of the narcotic of adulation which, throughout a friendless, charm-less and loveless thirty years of life, he had presumably craved at the deepest level. Wagner devotee that he was, he was natur-ally drawn to the politics of mass emotion. Not for him the quietly reasoned hope that by patient collaboration between men and women of good will, the worst features of the Treaty of Versailles could be negotiated; nor, at home, would he have possessed the smallest inclination to support a coalition of liberal opinion to safeguard jobs or institutional life as a more rational alternative to Bolshevism. From the very beginning, he wanted the big music of German nationalism, with all its associated xenophobia, philistine Jew-hatred and quasi-religious emotionalism. There were as many splinter parties of the extreme Right as there were of the extreme Left. As a much-trusted young speaker in the Aufklärungskommando, it was his task and his delight to sniff around in these unsavoury pools in Munich. He lighted upon the tiny German Workers Party, an extreme right-wing sect which had been founded by a Munich locksmith, Anton Drexler, on 7 March 1918. Drexler asked Hitler to join the central committee of the party, and he did so as the seventh member, though his membership number was 555. (It would seem unlikely that there were as many as 100, let alone 500, members at this date.) Karl Harrer, another of the party members, expressed the view, having heard committee member 555 speak in the Hofbräuhaus, one of the bigger beer-cellars in Munich, that Hitler had no gifts as an orator. But his opinion was not shared. The first time Hitler stood on the table of this medieval beer-hall and addressed the drinkers, there was an audience of 111. A little later, he addressed an audience of 200. By August 1920, the party was holding public rallies and had adopted the name by which it would ever afterwards be known – the National Socialist German Workers' Party. With the whimsical German habit of shortening, nicknames and acronymics, the supporters of the NSDAP – Nationalsozialistische Deutsche Arbeiterpartei – were called the Nazis.

Hitler's chief gift was for public speaking, but he also displayed, during these months, and in the years to come, two qualities which had lain latent and which, for example, his room-mate Kubizek could hardly have guessed at when he saw young Adolf lolling on his scruffy bed feeling sorry for himself in Vienna and doing absolutely nothing.

One of these gifts was a Machiavellian skill at political manipulation: it took him no time at all to move in on Drexler's little band of malcontents and make them accept him as their leader. The second thing which he brought to the party in particular, and to life in general, was a taste for violence. An essential colleague in Hitler's rise to power was Captain Ernst Röhm, a scar-faced homosexual who, as he said in the opening sentence of his memoirs, 'From my child-hood I had only one thought and wish – to be a soldier.' Röhm loved the company of mindlessly violent street-boys, and with the new party being organized by Hitler and friends, Röhm saw the perfect opportunity for rough stuff on the grand scale. When all-out mob violence was not available, there would always be shop windows to be smashed, Reds to be given bloody noses and Jews to be pummelled in darkened alleys. Röhm had organized a patriotic free army – Freikorps – of men coming out of the army who were determined to fight against the Communists. By bringing these men into the National Socialist movement from the beginning, Röhm not only swelled its ranks. He determined that it should be by definition a cult of violence. His storm-division, Sturmabteilung or SA, could march, in their brown shirts and

beneath the swastika emblem which had now been incorpor-
ated into the party regalia, as a private army within Germany.

Röhm attracted discontented ex-soldiers and violent
youths into his SA. This in turn made the Nazis, from their
inception, a frightening organization. If you criticized them
or fell foul of them for whatever reason, you knew that you
were risking broken ribs.

The intimidating power of his movement – and it had
become Hitler's movement from the moment he moved in on
Drexler's party – allowed him to develop his own cult of
personality. While the SA frightened his rivals, Hitler could
develop his quasi-operatic skills as a public performer.
Hitler's own gift for self-mythologizing was itself of a
Wagnerian capacity. 'In that hour, IT began.'

'It' – the thing which began with that production of *Rienzi*,
seen in his youth – was among other things a lifelong passion
for the music dramas of Richard Wagner. But it was also the
capacity to see himself, and politics, as part of a music drama.
He concluded the first volume of *My Struggle* with an account
of the first big National Socialist rally in Munich on 24
February 1920. What catches our attention here is not
whether any detail of Hitler's account is true or could be chal-
lenged by others, but the way in which he chose, in his book,
to present the occasion. He claimed that he alone took charge
of the organization of the rally. He advertised it with posters
and leaflets. 'The text was concise and definite, an absolutely
dogmatic form of expression being used.'[4] One of the aims of
the rally was to summon the faithful together. But another,

equally important to Hitler, was to antagonize the enemy. For this reason he chose to set the swastika emblem in red banners. The propaganda point which he wanted to make was that the centre parties in German politics were no more than useful stooges to the Communists. The effect which he wanted to produce by using red banners was to draw the Communists out for a street battle. He hoped that the police would try to ban his rally, because of the red banners, and that there would then be a pitched battle between National Socialists and Communists. He had an ally in the Chief of Police, Ernst Pöhner, 'who, in contradistinction to the majority of our so-called defenders of the authority of the State, did not fear to incur the enmity of traitors to the country and the nation but rather courted it as a mark of honour and honesty. For such men hatred of the Jews and Marxists and the lies and calumnies they spread, was their only source of happiness in the midst of national misery.'

Hitler tells us in *My Struggle* that as he strode into the crowds waiting outside the Hofbräuhaus for the rally, and saw over 2,000 people, 'my heart was nearly bursting with joy'.[5]

There were various speakers, some of whom were heckled. Then Hitler rose, and he proceeded to tell the audience of his twenty-five points. This was the party manifesto which Hitler and Drexler had thrashed out, including the ripping up of the Treaty of Versailles, the establishment of a Greater Germany formed by the union with Austria, and the abolition of Jewish rights of citizenship. As Hitler spoke on these themes, the hecklers fell silent, and his sentences were received with applause. For a speaker to outline twenty-five points, and to promise in advance that this was his intention, is, to put it mildly, asking a lot of an audience. Yet such was Hitler's magnetism that this deadly sounding speech clearly had the crowd in raptures. The meeting lasted four hours. 'As the masses streamed towards the exits, crammed shoulder to shoulder, shoving and pushing, I knew that a movement was now set afoot among the German people which would never pass into oblivion.'[6]

He saw it, however, in operatic terms. 'A fire was enkindled from whose glowing heat the sword would be fashioned which would restore freedom to the German Siegfried and bring back life to the German nation.'[7]

Henceforth, the German people were seen as an orchestra whom he could conduct, as a great chorus who could sing his compositions. During the two or three years after the war, the government in Berlin suffered many setbacks. Politicians, and political activists on the Left, continued to see Germany's problems in purely political terms. Hitler never did this. Kubizek as an adolescent had been surprised by Hitler's outburst after *Rienzi* because he had never heard him speak of politics before. We see no sign of politics as such interesting him throughout his twenties. As it happened, he would show consummate skill at political negotiation with those who thought, by their greater levels of sophistication or experience, that they could bamboozle or somehow use him. They would invariably find that he had wrong-footed them. For the time being, however, there was no need to paint in the details of his picture. He needed only the broad wash. Finer shading would come later.

In the summer of 1921, Hitler spent some time in Berlin among various nationalist groups and proposed a merger between the NSDAP and the German Socialist Party, run by Alfred Brunner, a Düsseldorf engineer, and the bullying anti-Semite Julius Streicher. When eyebrows were raised by his comrades in Munich, Hitler immediately threatened to resign – the last thing, by this stage, which the Munich nationalists could survive. The bumbling right-wing Bavarians were appalled by his behaviour, accusing Hitler of 'a lust for power and personal ambition'.[8] The character assessment was obviously true, even if their paranoid assertion that Hitler was being manipulated by the Jews was wide of the mark. He successfully sued the newspaper which printed this material. Drexler and Harrer were distressed, because they wanted to thrash out, point by point, where and how they might differ from Brunner and Streicher's German Socialist Party, and whether or not they were a fundamentally anti-capitalist organization. For Hitler, such divisive stuff was of no interest. He did not care for details. 'Any idea', he wrote in *My Struggle*, 'may be looked upon as a source of danger if it be looked upon as an end in itself …'[9]

Although Hitler's few ideas were in fact held very forcefully – international Jewish conspiracy, need for expansion into the East for *Lebensraum*, infallibility of Darwin's theories, and so forth – it never much troubled him if his ideas were self-contradictory. For example, he deplored both the financiers who manipulated international markets and the Bolsheviks who wished to overthrow them, and saw both of them as part of the same Jewish threat. What he had to offer was not a political programme but an opera, a black-hearted drama into which he wished to suck as many people as possible. Once they had heard it, and allowed its mad music to enter their souls, the German people would be spellbound. Discussion of detailed political ideas was always the undoing of little backstreet parties such as Drexler had founded. As Hitler himself later enunciated, it matters not how idiotic the creed. What matters is the firmness with which it is enunciated.[10] Nor was this viewpoint entirely cynical. Hitler had many faults, both as a man and as a politician. He was an incurable liar. He was brutal and cruel. He had none of the normal instincts of decency or kindliness. But he was not – as were some of the other Nazis who helped him into power, such as Goebbels or Speer – a cynical man. Although he distrusted almost everyone else – perhaps actually everyone – he believed in himself. And the great movement which he in some senses invented – embracing a national recovery based on poorly defined feelings of irrational uplift – actually depended for its success on its intellectual incoherence. He drew to himself those who hated Jews for being sinister men smoking cigars in boardrooms and bleeding Germany of its savings, and those who hated Jews for being red-eyed scavengers plotting the overthrow of capitalism and the manufacturing industry. He drew to himself those with a sense that he was protecting family values and religion, and those who thought – or rather felt – that he was the voice of the modern, the embodiment of Darwinian rationalism which had seen off religion. He drew to himself above all those who, through all the confused early years of the Weimar Republic, still felt the bitter wound of defeat in war, the dreadful unfairness of the Treaty, the sheer incredibility of the fact that the finest army in Europe, never defeated in the field, should have been written off as a failure – at the behest of a bespectacled Princeton professor, an unprincipled Welsh philandering liberal, and a deeply cynical old Frenchman who was determined to punish Germany for his own and his country's contemptible defeat by Prussia in 1870. To all these people Hitler offered the most tempting of Class A narcotics, that is, Hope. No wonder that on 29 July 1921, when he saw off his rivals and backbiting enemies in the tin-pot little NSDAP, there was first heard the description of him as *Unser Führer*: Our Leader.

THREE

1921–1923 My Struggle

Throughout the autumn of 1922, there were painful negotiations between Germany and the Allied powers about the
payment of reparations. The German Government pleaded
with the Allies but the French were adamant. Germany must
pay. When Germany defaulted, French troops moved into the
industrial Ruhr district on 11 January 1923. This was
Germany's industrial heartland. It accounted for eighty per
cent of the country's steel and pig-iron production and more
than eighty per cent of its coal.[1] With the paralysis, or effec-
tual confiscation, of German means of production, there was
even less chance of meeting the cruel French demands for
payment. The Germans adopted a policy of passive resistance
to the French.

The German mark lost its value on the international
currency markets. By 1 July, the rate of exchange with the
dollar had risen to 160,000 marks, by 1 August to a million,
by 1 November to 130,000 million. The ultimate capitalist
nightmare had fallen on the German middle classes. Their

savings were worth nothing. With inflation running at this level even the simplest commodities of life became unaffordable, and it really was the case that people needed a wheelbarrow to carry enough paper money to buy a simple week's groceries. Germany had been allowed, by the international community, to sink into a situation where there was no stability of any kind.

The army, in particular, and the ex-Freikorps officers, such as Ernst Röhm, favoured a military solution to the country's problems: a march on Berlin, and a war of revenge against the French. Hitler, who already had his sights on real political power, could see that such talk was nonsense. If they attempted to fight France yet again, they would be defeated. If, however, they fought the German Republican Government, and created the greatest possible mayhem, they could only be marching in the right direction – in the direction where power lay. To make their objectives too specific at this stage would be to risk defeat. He must be seen to move from triumph to triumph. At the same time, he must not be seen as a supporter of the status quo, so that illegal street fighting or fisticuffs with the Reds would do his reputation no harm at all.

By now Hitler was beginning to collect around him the grotesque gang of misfits and semi-criminals who would, for a nightmarish decade, be the most powerful political clique in Europe. There was Julius Streicher, whose shaven head was an ugly pink sea urchin. This short, stocky primary school teacher ran a newspaper, *Der Stürmer*, with a line in anti-

Jewish fantasy lurid even by the standards of southern Germany. The pages of *Der Stürmer* reflected a mind which was filled with bandy-legged Jews seducing pure German maidens, and money-grubbing Jews eating or murdering Christian babies.

Then there was the preposterous figure of Hermann Göring, a pampered, overweight kleptomaniac. He loved uniforms and when the Nazis achieved power, he appeared in ever more fantastical Ruritanian costumes, with epaulettes the dimension of elaborate Bavarian pastries, and rows of medals. He had been a flying ace in the war, which gave him contact with members of the aristocracy. He was more 'class' than most other members of the movement, a fact which in the initial stages gave him a certain clout. When Lord Halifax met him in 1936 he said that he was 'a composite personality – film star, great landowner interested in his estate, prime minister, party manager, head gamekeeper at Chatsworth'.[2]

On May Day 1923 there was a peaceful march by the socialists through the centre of Munich. Hitler, clad in a steel helmet and wearing his Iron Cross, which he had won for being, in effect, little more than an obedient postman, accompanied by Göring, and a group of others – Hess, Streicher and Strasser – stood ready to lead 20,000 storm-troopers (SA) to break up the socialists. But at the agreed signal, Captain Röhm did not come to their help. It was a serious humiliation to Hitler. His SA troops handed back their arms to the local army barracks. Meanwhile, in Berlin, the economic and political situation worsened. Wilhelm Cuno resigned as Chancellor to be replaced by Gustav Stresemann. There were strikes. There were riots by Communists. Trains and trucks were regularly raided by the hungry. The country was more or less in a state of anarchy.

On 2 September 1922, the anniversary of the defeat of France at Sedan in 1870, there was a huge demonstration in Nuremberg presided over by General Ludendorff, the distinguished old war general. On 26 September, Stresemann announced that the government was calling off the passive resistance plan and pleaded once more for a negotiated settlement with the French. Hitler put his own 15,000 stormtroopers on alert.

The State Governor in Munich, Gustav von Kahr, asked for, and received, Hitler's solemn assurance that he was not planning an anti-government putsch. There followed one of Hitler's characteristically whopping lies. The world would get used to these, and the more extreme the lie, the more decent people, such as Lord Halifax and Neville Chamberlain, would feel inclined to believe them. 'Never as long as I live', Hitler told Kahr, 'would I make a putsch.'

At the beginning of October, it looked as if Kahr was heading for a major confrontation with the Berlin government. Stresemann and his liberal-socialist Cabinet expressed the desire to close down the scurrilous right-wing Bavarian newspaper, the in effect Nazi *Völkischer Beobachter* (The Nazi Observer – the word '*völkisch*' meaning literally 'of the people' came to stand for the whole bundle of patriotic or nationalist feelings which the Nazis represented). They also wanted to replace the right-wing General Otto von Lossow as leader of the army in Bavaria and put General Kress von Kressenstein in his stead. This set of proposals delighted Hitler by causing violently anti-government feelings to be aroused in otherwise moderate Bavarians. '*Auf nach Berlin!*' – 'On to Berlin!' – became a nationalist watchword.

But then Stresemann's government appeared to be on top of things. They broke the threat of a Communist uprising. General Müller suppressed the governments of Saxony and Thuringia, which had the effect of strengthening central power and was designed *pour encourager les autres*. Colonel Hans Ritter von Seisser warned Hitler and the Bavarian would-be rebels that, in the event of a putsch, there was no hope that malcontents in the north of the country would join it.

By now it was too late. Hitler had already primed his followers, telling them that he would take part in a putsch. On 8 November Kahr was due to speak to a sympathetic right-ring audience in the Bürgerbräukeller or Citizen's Beer Hall. Twenty minutes after Kahr had begun to speak, Hitler, Göring and twenty-five armed Brownshirts burst into the building.

One symptom of Hitler's being strangely at variance with reality, or the nature of things, was his gift for wearing inappropriate or ludicrous clothing. Even if you overlook his fondness for lederhosen and knee-length pale socks, his dress sense was, to put it mildly, uncertain. On this occasion, when he was supposed to be starting a militaristic revolution, he was wearing evening dress and an ill-fitting black tailcoat, which reminded one observer of 'the slightly nervous sort of provincial bridegroom you can see in scores of pictures behind the dusty windows of Bavarian village photographers',[3] and his army medals. He fired a revolver in the air and shouted, 'The National revolution is begun!' It was Hitler's aim to persuade Kahr, and the army, supported by Ludendorff, to march on Berlin, and overthrow the left-wing government. Any such adventure would have been doomed to end in failure, and Kahr had no intention of going along with the Nazi plans. Kahr behaved unflappably. 'You can arrest me or shoot me. Whether I die or not is no matter.' Colonel Seisser reproached Hitler for so flagrantly breaking his word. 'Yes, I did', admitted Hitler. 'Forgive me. I had to, for the sake of the Fatherland.'[4] He then announced that the Berlin government had been overthrown and that Herr von Kahr was the 'Regent' – not an honour which he accepted. But the crowd liked it. Hitler's announcement that they had replaced the Berlin government was greeted with applause.

Two Hitlers were on display that evening. One was the strutting populist revolutionary demagogue, thirsting for the applause of the crowd. But his sense of timing had deserted him, and he knew that this coup d'état was not going to happen. So there was seen that other Hitler, the cringing lower middle-class man who felt ill at ease with his social or military superiors and would do all in his oleaginous power to be ingratiating. Almost bowing to Kahr, he said, 'If your Excellency permits, I will drive out to see His Majesty [that is the Bavarian Crown Prince Rupprecht] at once and inform him that the German people have arisen and made good the injustice done to His Majesty's late lamented father.'

Kahr agreed that this should be done. But he had no intention of bowing to Hitler's pressure. He and his Cabinet withdrew during the night to Regensburg where they continued the legal government of Bavaria. General Lossow returned to barracks, where the commander of the Munich garrison, General Danner, asked drily, 'All that was bluff, your Excellency?' The next day, Hitler and General Ludendorff returned to the Bürgerbräukeller with a column of Nazi storm-troopers. They were met, not by the army, which would have provided too great a clash of loyalty in some storm-troopers' hearts, but by the police. In the exchange of gunfire, which lasted only a minute or so, sixteen Nazis were killed and three police. Göring was wounded and smuggled across the Austrian border and given hospital treatment at the expense of the Wagners. Hitler suffered a dislocated shoulder.

A few days after the attempted putsch, Hitler was arrested.

If Hitler had been an inhabitant of the rational world, the world of John Locke or Abraham Lincoln, the ridiculous putsch of 1923 would have been seen as an abject and humiliating exposure of weakness. But he lived in strange times, and he had an altogether anti-rational take on events.

Hitler made his trial a piece of drama. General Lossow was the man who did not survive the trial. He emerged as a Prince Hamlet, unable to decide whether he had or had not supported the Nazis and their putsch. 'The well-known eloquence of Herr Hitler at first made a strong impression on me, but the more I heard of him, the fainter this impression became. I realized that his long speeches were always about the same thing, that his views were partly a matter-of-course for any German of nationalist views, and partly showed that Hitler lacked a sense of reality and the ability to see what was possible and practical.'[5]

Exactly. Which was why Hitler, in the topsy-turvy world of the Weimar Republic, was going to succeed and why Lossow was on the heap. Lossow accused Hitler of personal ambition, and said that he was a mere 'drummer'. While attempting to subdue the infuriating Hitler he had in fact given the great diva his cue for a magnificent aria in the court room –

> 'How petty are the thoughts of small men! Believe me, I do not regard the acquisition of a minister's portfolio as a thing worth striving for. I do not think it worthy of a great man to endeavour to go down in history just by becoming a minister …'[6]

So, Hitler, the thirty-four-year-old down-and-out failed art-student who had never achieved anything at all in his life, was now the 'great man'. The judge, the lawyers, the generals, and the elected politicians in the court room were the also-rans. It was a useful lesson for them to learn.

Revealingly, Hitler did not compare himself to Bismarck, still less to Kahr or Lossow or to any of the political figures in

German history. No, he took his audience in spirit to stand beside the grave of the Master.

> When I stood for the first time at the grave of Richard Wagner my heart overflowed with pride in a man who had forbidden any such inscription as: Here lies Privy Councillor, Music-Director, His Excellency Baron Richard von Wagner. I was proud that this man and so many others in German history were content to give their names to history without titles. It was not from modesty that I wanted to be a drummer in those days. That was the highest aspiration: the rest is nothing.
>
> The man who is born to be a dictator is not compelled; he wills it. He is not driven forward, but drives himself. There is nothing immodest about this. Is it immodest for a worker to drive himself towards heavy labour? Is it presumptuous of a man with a high forehead of a thinker to ponder through the nights till he gives the world an invention? The man who feels called upon to govern a people, has no right to say: if you want me, or summon me, I will co-operate. No, it is his duty to step forward.[7]

It was a strange defence. He had taken part in a failed attempt at the violent overthrow of the legal government. His response was that he was a great man, an imaginative genius in the tradition of a great composer, a national saviour.

In an English court, Hitler would have been asked whether he had, or had not, planned the putsch; whether he had, or had not, attempted to overthrow the legitimate government of his country; whether he had, or had not, urged his followers to shoot policemen. In Bavaria, 1923, Hitler was given a prison sentence of five years, and sent to the fortress prison of Landsberg. From this perspective in time, it might be thought that he would have emerged from the court room as a ridiculous failure who had been guilty of sedition and mind-bogglingly absurd *folie de grandeur*. On the contrary, at the time, he was seen by thousands of admirers as a hero. Far from laughing at his claim to be Germany's natural dictator, who was merely waiting for the moment when Destiny called, they took him completely seriously. And it was less than a decade before Destiny would comply.

Hitler's fortress prison was scarcely penitential. Winifred Wagner, Richard Wagner's daughter-in-law and an early supporter, sent pencil and papers urging him to write a great tract, or his memoirs. She also supplied him with hampers of delicious foods, as did many other faithful followers. Hitler was allowed an airy upstairs room, comfortably furnished, with a clear view of rolling countryside. Dressed in lederhosen, he could loll in a comfortable armchair, attended by the devout Rudolf Hess, the heavily eyebrowed earnest figure, besotted from the beginning by Hitler's personality, and who was allowed the privilege of answering the letters and arranging the flowers sent to Landsberg by the faithful. Hess spoke at this time of the way that Hitler radiated 'something that puts those around him under its spell and spreads in ever-widening circles'.[8] Ridiculous as Hess might seem to posterity, he spoke no less than the truth. Whether we like to admit it or not, Hitler did have this mesmeric force. Before the catastrophic end, millions had felt its dark, hypnotic strength.

To the faithful Hess fell the sacred task of typing out the Leader's great book, *My Struggle*. For, although Winifred Wagner imagined her hero sitting busily at his table and filling notebooks with his wisdom, he in fact preferred speaking to writing.

It is a curious work. We have already indicated that the title is one of its fictitious aspects. True, it was a misfortune that his parents had died early. The rest of the struggle is less easy to identify. The grinding poverty came about simply from Hitler's personal fecklessness, and not because he had lived through an economic crisis. As for the downfall of Greater Germany and the defeat of both Germany and Austria in the World War, while he took these things intensely personally, they were phenomena which affected persons other than himself.

But you would never guess so from reading *My Struggle*. The British novelist Anthony Powell used to say that self-pity was an essential ingredient in any bestseller and to this extent, the self projected through the pages of *My Struggle* is one with mass appeal.

The political programme which it advances is one from which Hitler deviated very little over the next twenty years, though he was compelled to modify his expressed belief that Britain would be his ally, or at best a neutral partner in the programme of Teutonic world domination which he outlined.

He said that Germany was either a great world power or it was nothing. It would become a great world power again when it waged war in the East and took *Lebensraum* from the Russians. Those responsible for the tragedy of German defeat in the war must be held to account. These were the Communists and, often the same people, the Jews. The sacrifice of millions in the battlefields at the Front would not have been necessary if 'twelve or fifteen thousand of these Hebrew corrupters had been held under poison gas'.

It is a baffling fact that so many historians of Hitler continue to speak belittlingly of *My Struggle* as a key text explaining his later intentions. We must not suppose, they say, that when he speaks of gassing the Jews in *My Struggle*, he already had in mind a Final Solution. Maybe not, but the intention was plain enough. And this was the book which was freely available throughout Germany during all the years of his increased popularity. No one can say that his followers did not know what he was advocating. Likewise, we are told that the Germans were all shocked when Hitler led the world into a war. Very likely they were. But by then, there had been sixteen years in which to read his book, in which he repetitively harangues the reader with the necessity of war, its cleansing effects and its inevitability after the perfidy of Versailles and the actions of the November criminals.

So, although it is in many ways a boring book, *My Struggle* is also one of stupendous historical importance. Other men write their autobiography when they have passed through their great life-experiences. Hitler wrote his autobiography as a manifesto of what he wanted to do. The Struggle was one which he believed himself to have passed through. But in another sense, the clever title is an indication of what is to come.

Over 500 visitors came to Landsberg Prison to see him, including General Ludendorff himself. The very act of being imprisoned, as other great political demagogues have discovered since in imitation of Hitler, was a very useful career move. It was now felt among the extreme Right that no move forward was possible without Hitler. That Struggle, or Fight – in German the same thing, *Kampf* – was not a reference to Hitler's inability to buy a decent suit of clothes or sell his lousy postcard paintings in the back-streets of Vienna in the years before the war. The Struggle/Fight lay ahead. It was the fight for the future identity of Germany. If he were successful, it would be a fight for the future identity of the world itself.

FOUR

1923–1929 The Politics of Catastrophe

'I guarantee you', Hitler proclaimed, 'that the impossible always succeeds. What is unlikeliest is surest.'[1] Certainly, as he emerged from Landsberg Prison, it would have seemed unlikely, if not impossible, to most analysts of his situation, that he was within rather less than nine years of becoming the Chancellor of Germany. 'For me and for all of us', he said on another occasion, 'setbacks have been only the whiplash which drove us onward with more determination than before.'[2]

Had he been a regular politician, there is no doubt that he would have vanished without trace after the prison experience. By the time he emerged from Landsberg, the party which he had led had shattered into many fissiparous and quarrelsome groups. There was no party funding, no party discipline, and, what was worse from the point of view of these right-wing malcontents, the Weimar Republic began to enjoy a period of comparative stability. Hitler was not a politician. Politics have been called the 'art of the possible'. Hitler dealt with the art of the impossible. He was more a mage or a conjuror than a politician. Politics are the method of governing a country by some process of reason. The debate is: how. As Lenin asked: Who whom? Who would control whom? Who would control the economy? Who, if anyone, would attempt to control the market? Obviously when Hitler did eventually assume control of Germany, he would be compelled to address these political questions. Patient politicians of the Weimar Republic had to deal with the day-to-day movements of world markets, the grind of international diplomacy, the economic problems of unemployment. Politicians watched the weather and waited for calm. Hitler wanted to ride storms.

In the five years after he left prison, however, the skies over Germany slowly cleared and it looked as if no storms would come. In 1924 an international committee headed by the American banker Charles G. Dawes proposed a system of foreign loans which would make the repayment of reparations conceivable. The currency stabilized with the introduction of the Rentenmark. The politicians, or would-be politicians, of the *völkisch* Right did not enjoy much success. Franconia and Bavaria, their supposed heartland, produced a dwindling of votes at elections. In the course of one year nearly 70 per cent of their following had evaporated.[3]

The next five years saw no great advance for the Nazis. It was a time, however, for Hitler, when he began to collect about him some of the companions who would make his success, when it came, so stupendous. One of these followers was Gregor Strasser, a pharmacist from Landshut. A great big man, who enjoyed pub brawls, he was also one who enjoyed reading Homer in Greek, and who was a great phrase-maker. It was Strasser who saw clearly that Nazism could only succeed on the back of Germany's failure. It needed not just setbacks but the worst of times to stimulate its desperate purposes. 'We will attain everything if we set hunger, despair and sacrifice marching for our aims', he said. He saw nationalist and socialist despair flaming in 'a single great fire'. Here was a man after Hitler's own Schopenhauerian heart. He advocated 'the politics of catstrophe',[4] and if there is one phrase which sums up Hitler's credo, it was this. Schopenhauer and Strasser had only despair in their souls. For Hitler, with his craving for adulation, however, despair was only a means to an end. Riding on the storms of Germany's despair, he wanted to be able to bring salve and cure, to be hailed as the Saviour. He had been denied the chance to save Germany by armed revolution. He could now only hope to do so through the ballot box. And no sane German would vote for the politics of catastrophe until, once more, they lived in catastrophic times.

Strasser, the leading light of the Berlin radical Right, would not last long in the Nazi movement. He insisted that its anti-Bolshevist prejudice was wrong and that they should aim for a socialist transformation of society. Someone who took the opposite view was Strasser's colleague Joseph Goebbels. This extraordinarily unpleasant person, who physically resembled Nosferatu the Vampyre of film legend, came from Rheydt, a small industrial town in the Elberfeld area of the Ruhr. Born in 1897, Goebbels had been educated at Catholic boarding schools, but his faith did not survive beyond childhood. Osteomyelitis rendered him lame, and he had to wear a metal brace on his leg and a block shoe. His condition had in fact rendered him unfit for military service. A shameless liar, he had no compunction about suggesting that his limping gait was caused by war wounds. The fact that he was only five foot in height did not deflect his energy as a determined amorist: one of the many ways in which he differed from Hitler. It was the French occupation of the Ruhr region which radicalized Goebbels. His Ph.D. and his aspirations to be a poet, playwright or novelist made him seem like the intellectual of the movement, but he was no more a writer than Hitler was a painter. The fact that both had attempted success in their various creative fields and both had abjectly failed only increased the bitterness with which they looked out upon the world.

In 1925–6 it looked likely that the northern Nazis, dominated by Strasser and Goebbels, would take precedence over the madder rabble in Munich, and that Hitler would be superseded. Strasser was appalled, for example, by the low-grade quality of the *Völkischer Beobachter*. Goebbels wrote in his diary, 'Nobody has faith in Munich any more.'[5] But when Hitler began to visit Berlin, he learnt how to woo Goebbels at Strasser's expense. 'He pampers me like a child', Goebbels told his diary.

Lord Beaverbrook once said that the way to run a successful newspaper was to put a ferret in the cage. What he meant by this was that if he appointed to his staff an individual whom the editor hated, the creative tension would produce interesting results. It would also leave both in a position of subordination to the proprietor. Hitler was a master of the ferret in the cage technique of man-management. As NSDAP leader, he appointed Strasser as head of propaganda. But he then made Goebbels the new Gauleiter, or district leader, of the capital. The Berlin Nazis were thereby locked in a situation by which both their leading figures would be at loggerheads. Hitler made the two friends into enemies.

Goebbels and Hitler during these quiescent years of the party's history laid the foundations of its future success. Hitler made it his object to suppress dissent. The debates which Strasser and the other northern Nazis wished to have about the exactitudes of party doctrine were forbidden. Was the party pro-capitalist, or anti-capitalist? Surely, Strasser argued, it could not be both. Hitler responded that one of the great secrets of Christianity's success was the unalterability of its dogmas.[6] This demonstrated at least two things: Hitler's ignorance of the ever-changing pattern of Christian history, and his determination to impose a discipline upon his party as intolerant as that of the nineteenth-century popes upon the church of his baptism.

In July 1926, he and Goebbels organized a mass rally in Weimar. Hitler, dressed in a belted tunic and puttees, addressed 5,000 people. Some said the performance was somewhat lacklustre. This was the first time that Hitler upraised his hand in a Roman salute, in the gesture which would soon become so familiar to his followers. The time would come when not 5,000 but a whole nation would return the salute with the cry of 'Heil Hitler!' But on this occasion, there was flatness. Only the hard core of the old *völkisch* Right had turned up. Gregor Strasser remarked on this occasion that National Socialism was dead.[7]

These were years of party retrenchment and reorganization, of waiting in the doldrums, waiting either for a helpful catastrophe, or, from a Nazi perspective, a disastrous progress towards national stability. They were also years in which Hitler appears in the company of women. Hitherto, the only women of note in his life had been his mother and a girl named Stefanie, loved from afar in Linz, and to whom he had not plucked up courage to speak. In his post-war celebrity as a speaker, he attracted female patrons. One of the earliest to join the NSDAP, even before the Munich putsch, had been Winifred Wagner, the Welsh daughter-in-law of the Master, a person with whom Hitler established an instantaneous rapport when they first met at the Golden Anchor Hotel in Bayreuth. The meeting occurred in 1923, when Hitler was thirty-four and she an attractive twenty-six-year-old. From the first, she bid him call her Winnie, and he asked her to use his pet name of Wolf. Albert Speer, the young architect who was destined to become one of Hitler's closest associates, once told the historian Joachim Fest that Hitler and Winnie had been lovers at some point. Whether or not this was true, Winnie provided Hitler with something he had sorely lacked all his life – a family circle. Hitler stayed regularly with

Winnie, her husband the composer and conductor Siegfried Wagner and her four children, who looked on the Leader as a benign uncle and family friend. In the Wagners' company, clearly, Hitler was always on best behaviour. They did not see him rant or use foul language or lose his temper.

Family life was also on offer in the company of the Hanfstaengls. Catherine Hanfstaengl, an American by birth and of liberal political inclinations, had been bowled over very early by Hitler's oratorical magic, and by the Wagnerian idea of a young man from nowhere arriving as the saviour. She was a noted Munich *salonnière* and it was in her house that Hitler met many of his rich backers for the first time. People noticed his sycophancy; the manner, for example, when talking to General Ludendorff, of raising his bottom with a half bow at the old man's every sentence – 'Very well, your Excellency!' 'Quite so, your Excellency!'[8] Catherine's son Ernst, known as Putzi, became Hitler's friend, and he has left us some of the most vivid impressions of what it was like to be in the Leader's presence: his habit of farting in cars, for example; or the way in which the oleaginous social manner could suddenly fall away, and an outburst like Tourette's syndrome could burst through, as when, on one occasion, someone let fall a friendly remark about the Jews, and Hitler thrust back his chair, stood up and suddenly started yelling. These accounts of Hitler in the salon conjure up a mixture of amusement and horror, comparable to those scenes in Dostoyevksy's *The Devils*, when the nihilist murderer/pervert Stavrogin misbehaves in his mother's drawing room. In fact,

one sees that Dostoyevsky with his prescient imagination has painted a horrifying tragic-comedy of what happens
when an intelligent bourgeoisie sells its soul to a monster.
Thinking to patronize him, these fools – both the fictitious
ones in the pages of the Russian novel, and the actual friends
of Hitler – have no idea that the 'interesting' figure they are
hosting has a gigantic – to use one of his own favourite adjec-
tives – demonic power; that they are his puppets, rather than
he theirs.

Another woman who made it her mission to civilize Hitler
was Frau Bechstein, the wife of the celebrated piano manu-
facturer. She lent all her jewels, valued at 60,000 Swiss francs,
as a surety which enabled Hitler to borrow money from a
Berlin coffee merchant for much-needed party funds.[9] She
tried to teach him table manners and normal social graces,
and at one of her soirées, when she had managed to persuade
the teetotalling Leader to hold a glass of wine in his hand
like everyone else, she was appalled to witness him calling
over a servant with a sugar bowl, and scooping in a lump or
two to make the grown-up drink acceptable to his childish
palate.

Certainly, snobs found his intrusion into the houses of the
rich disconcerting. The aristocratic misanthrope Friedrich
Reck-Malleczewen was undoubtedly one such, but his
account of what the Nazis did to his country, in his posthu-
mously published *Diary of a Man in Despair*, is, once read,
unforgettable. Reck-Malleczewen first encountered Hitler at
the house of his friend Clemens von Franckenstein who was

not a mad scientist as his name implies, but a musical composer and the director of the Bavarian Court Theatre. This was back in 1920. Hitler had forced his way into Franckenstein's house alleging that he had come to discuss the design of sets for operas. When Reck-Malleczewen arrived at the house, the butler complained to him that Hitler had already been there an hour:

> He had come to a house, where he had never been before, wearing gaiters, a floppy, wide-brimmed hat, and carrying a riding whip. There was a German Shepherd dog, too. The effect, among the Gobelin tapestries and cool marble walls, was something akin to a cowboy's sitting down on the steps of a baroque altar in leather breeches, spurs, and with a Colt at his side. But Hitler sat there, the stereotype of a headwaiter – at that time, he was thinner, and looked somewhat starved – both impressed and restricted by the presence of a real, live Herr Baron; awed, not quite daring to sit fully in his chair, but perched on half, more or less, of his thin loins; not caring at all that there was a great deal of cool and elegant irony in the things his host said to him, but snatching hungrily at the words, like a dog at pieces of raw meat.
>
> Eventually he managed to launch into a speech. He talked on and on, endlessly. He preached. He went on and on at us like a division chaplain in the Army. We did not in the least contradict him or venture to differ in any way, but he began to bellow at us. The servants thought we were being attacked, and rushed in to defend us.

When he had gone, we sat silently confused and not at all amused. There was a feeling of dismay, as when on a train you suddenly find you are sharing a compartment with a psychotic. We sat a long time and no one spoke. Finally, Cle stood up, opened one of the huge windows, let the warm spring air into the room. It was not that our grim guest had been unclean, and fouled the room in the way that so often happens in a Bavarian village. But the fresh air helped to dispel the feeling of oppression. It was not that an unclean body had been in the room, but something else: the unclean essence of a monstrosity.[10]

In 1926, Hitler had a Bavarian holiday with his gang of cronies in the Obersalzberg, the stupendous mountain scenery which will forever, thanks to his presence there, possess a rather sinister atmosphere. High in the mountains above Berchtesgaden, he stayed at the Pension Moritz, whose owners, the Büchners, were admirers, and it was while there that he took the lease on the Haus Wachenfeld. It belonged to a Berlin businessman's widow – born Wachenfeld. The modest 100 marks a month were paid by yet another admirer, and he was eventually enabled to buy the property, transforming it into his vast mountain eyrie, a modern place known as the Berghof, or Mountain Court. Here indeed was a dream-place, a fantasy-residence worthy of the magician Klingsor.

'When I go to Obersalzberg, I'm not drawn there merely by the beauty of the landscape', he once told his friends. 'I feel myself far from petty things, and my imagination is stimulated. When I study a problem elsewhere, I see it less clearly, I'm submerged by the details. By night, at the Berghof, I often remain for hours with my eyes open, contemplating from my bed the mountains lit up by the moon. It is at such moments that brightness enters my mind.'[11]

It was during one of his stays in Berchtesgaden that Hitler met Maria Reiter, always known as Mimi. She was sixteen; he was thirty-seven. Blonde, submissive, prepared to dote upon him and cover him with adulation, she was 'my dear child' to him; he was 'Wolf', an exciting authoritative figure who now often carried a whip and wore knee-length boots. Now that he had backers, and the hope of some regular life, he had begun the practice, which he retained to the end of his days, of keeping a dog. The current German Shepherd, known as Prinz, picked a fight with Mimi's Marco – a dog of the same breed. Hitler gave Prinz a good thrashing with his whip, which clearly excited Mimi. It is to be assumed that they were lovers. When Hitler grew in fame and notoriety rumours circulated about his sexuality. The popular song during the Second World War, set to the tune of *Colonel Bogey*, was that

Hitler has only got one ball –[12]

This was not true. His doctors reported that all was normal in that area. At various stages, he was accused of crypto-homosexuality; of coprophilia; or the inability to penetrate women normally, and so on. In fact, it would seem as if

Hitler's sexuality was all but normal. Clearly in his early years he had been painfully shy in all areas of life. When Friedelind Wagner – the 'black sheep' of the family, who grew up as an anti-Nazi and went to live in America to escape the madness of her mother's Nazism – once shocked the family table by asking, at her fifteenth birthday dinner, 'Will someone please tell me what "prostitution" means?' silence fell on the table, until her mother's lover, Tietjen, asked, 'Where did you read that word?' 'In *Mein Kampf*. I have just finished it,' Friedelind replied. She pointed out that there were at least ten pages devoted to the subject. She tried the same trick with a school-mistress, this time asking the meaning of the word 'syphilis' and saying she had read it first in *My Struggle*. The book does indeed reveal a morbid fear of syphilis, which has led some to suppose that he had some unfortunate experience with a prostitute in Vienna. But syphilis was a terrifying illness in the pre-penicillin world, and when one thinks of the wide-spread devastation it caused, there was nothing surprising about an advanced hypochondriac such as Hitler having a morbid fear of it.

His domestic life in Munich was settling down. In 1928, he telephoned his half-sister Angela Raubal in Vienna and asked her to come to the Magic Mountain and to keep house for him. She brought her daughter with her, a sixteen-year-old girl called Geli. Hitler now spent as much time as possible in his mountain retreat. In 1929, rich benefactors enabled him to acquire a substantial nine-room apartment in Munich, 16 Prinzregentenstrasse. Geli was obsessed by the theatre, and came with him to Munich in order to take lessons in singing and acting. Almost from the beginning, there was gossip about the intimacy between Hitler and his niece. Undoubtedly, his relationship with her was intense, passionate, perhaps as intense as any in his entire life. No one knows quite what form it took, and whether there was an explicitly sexual element in it. Given the fact that Hitler's own mother had married a man who was all but her uncle, there would have been family precedent for some level of incest. If your mother had habitually called your father 'uncle', you might well fall in love with your niece.

But as political and economic life in Germany stabilized, Hitler's public backing began to diminish. When he addressed a rally in Munich in April 1927, the crowd had shrunk to 1,500. The Bavarian police were reporting that by 1928, branch meetings of the Nazi Party which might have been attended by 300–400 people in 1926 now attracted only 50 or 60 people.[13]

It was essential, in these conditions of apathy, to attempt to rally the faithful. From 1 to 4 August 1929 in Nuremberg, the great medieval mercantile centre of southern Germany, with its beautiful Gothic churches, its market-places, and its cherished House of Albrecht Dürer, Goebbels and Hitler decided to revive the party with a grand spectacle. The party membership all over Germany was just about 130,000. Not many when spread about the country, but if assembled in one spot, they would still seem 'gigantic'. Hitler asked everyone of influence whom he had known during these doldrum years

– Winifred Wagner came from Bayreuth, from the Ruhr came industrialist Emil Kirdorf. Thirty-five special trains brought SA (the Sturmabteilung, the storm-division, the Nazi street army) and SS men (the elite Schutzstaffel, or guard detachment, the hard core of Nazi Grail Knights) from all over Germany. The police reckoned that as many as 40,000 people were assembled in one place. There were floats, parades, torch-lit processions, and speeches by the Leader which were received with rapture.[14]

Hitler had by now achieved one of his aims, and these doldrum years were the essential period in which to achieve it: namely, total domination of the National Socialist Party and of the *völkisch* movement in general. This 1929 Nuremberg Rally set the seal on that achievement.

Goebbels and Hitler had set the stage. All that was now needed was thunder and lightning from the wings. For that they were dependent upon the cruel gods of the northern theogony, on the incestuous Wotan, on the furious Thor with his hammer, and on the mad dragons who guarded the gold-hoards. These unseen divinities did not disappoint. On 3 October 1929, Gustav Stresemann, the only truly statesman-like figure in the Weimar Republic, died of a stroke. Three weeks later, on 24 October, in an entirely disconnected calamity, the New York Stock Market collapsed. The implosion of world capitalism, so long awaited by catastrophe politicians of Left and Right, had finally happened.

Strangely, the Nazis were slow to recognize the significance of this event in America. The *Völkischer Beobachter* did not even mention it in its next issue. But the effects of the crash on the worldwide economy, and on Germany in particular, could not be hidden from anyone. By January 1930, 14 per cent of the adult workforce were unemployed: the labour exchanges recorded 3,218,000 unemployed but the true figure was much greater, probably nearer 4.5 million.[15]

Free society was failing.

FIVE

1929–1933 'A Simple Cowherd can become a Cardinal'

'Instead of working to take power by force, we must hold our noses and enter the Reichstag against the Catholic and Marxist deputies', Hitler had said after he came out of prison in 1924. Far from his party finding it easy to attract votes while its anti-democratic leadership held their noses, they failed to attract the electorate.

After the death of Stresemann, leader of the National Liberal Party, and the Wall Street Crash, everything was different. The German Government broke up in March 1930 and from then until Hitler became Chancellor in January 1933, majority government was impossible. The Centre Left had failed. The President, Field Marshal Paul von Hindenburg, appointed as Chancellor the leader of the Catholic Centre Right party, Heinrich Brüning. He dissolved the Reichstag and thereby inadvertently began the process which would allow the Nazis to achieve power. In the elections which followed, Hitler hoped that his Nazis might win sixty seats in the Reichstag. He won 107, and the Nazis now held about one-fifth of the Reichstag. Brüning, who regarded National Socialism as 'a feverish phenomenon', offered Hitler a role in a coalition with the socialists. The offer was of course refused. The government which Brüning had managed to cobble together then proceeded to institute a number of emergency decrees which were both highly unpopular and ineffectual. Wages were cut, unemployment pay was cut, women were dismissed from public employment. When he visited Breslau in 1932, the crowd pelted Brüning with stones. Unemployment soared to 6 million and continued to rise. The working classes hated Brüning. The employers hated him, because he tried to impose a freeze on price rises. The next year, 1932, there were two elections in which the Nazis picked up a yet larger share of the votes.

Hitler was riding the storm, and would eventually come to power by something very close to a democratic process. He very nearly came unstuck through a tragic scandal. On 18 September 1931, when Hitler was criss-crossing the country in an election journey, he received the news that his niece, Geli Raubal, had committed suicide in the Munich flat. It would seem that no other event – not even the death of his mother – affected him as this did. She had shot herself with Hitler's revolver. All kinds of theories have been advanced. Some suggest that she was having an affair with a Jew and that she was murdered by Nazis to avoid this 'scandal'. Others have supposed that Nazis murdered her because the peculiar nature of the relationship with her uncle was going to be exposed by blackmailers. Others have imagined what is probably the truth, that, for whatever reason, the poor young woman had had enough of living and did indeed take her own life.

Hitler was completely devastated. Just as, when life was going well for him, he became hyper-energetic and over-excited, so, when setbacks occurred, he was thrown into despair. He said that he wished to give up political life. In all the years which followed, it was forbidden by Hitler's entourage to mention Geli's name in his presence. If Geli did inadvertently crop up in the conversation, his eyes always filled with tears. He was truly devastated. A bust of her was placed in the room where she killed herself and for year on year, on the anniversary of her death, Hitler would shut himself in her room for hours on end. Before he left her for the last time, there had been a violent row between uncle and niece. She had wanted to cut loose and go for a while to Vienna, a scheme to which he was implacably opposed. To what extent this triggered her death, we shall probably never know.

Scandal-mongers churned out filth about Hitler and his niece, inventing lurid sexual perversions which the uncle and niece had shared. But there is always the possibility that they were simply very fond of one another. The British poet Stevie Smith, who led a maidenly existence, unmarried, in a dull suburb north of London, once angrily reacted to a person who told her she did not have any experience of love. 'I do', she replied. 'I love my aunt'. Love takes many forms.

After Geli's suicide, servants were engaged to fill the vacuum. Rosa Mitterer became a maid in the flat, and later at the Berghof. At first when she was engaged by Hitler, she would hear him weeping through the ceiling. Her first task each day, when up in the mountains, was to feed Hitler's dogs: first Prinz and then two other German Shepherds, Muckl or Muck and Wolf. Her verdict, delivered sixty years later, matched that of almost everyone else who worked for him: 'He was a charming man, someone who was only ever nice to me, a great boss to work for. You can say what you like but he was a good man to us.' Hitler, who was deliberately to engineer the deaths of millions, and who ranted at generals and politicians, was habitually gentle with servants and secretaries.

The death of Geli broke Hitler. It also strengthened his other great love – for the crowds. And when it became clear that he was capable of rallying from the sorrow of bereavement, he was able to throw himself even more fervently into his role as the National Saviour – one which, however cynically it was manipulated by Goebbels and the party machine, was one in which Hitler to all appearances passionately and sincerely believed. The very beginning of his political career – as a rabble-rousing speaker in the army at the end of the First World War – had been preceded by a collapse. From the depths of depression, and, as he would have us believe, actual blindness, he rose to a mysterious energy. There were many of these minor falls and rises in his bipolar emotional-political career. But the crisis after the death of Geli was the most profound. Her loss took him to the depths of despair. Thereafter, he rose to a new demonic energy, and there would be no stopping him.

As well as being the time of political advancement for the party on the national scene, it was also the time when the party finalized its own readiness for government.

Much is sometimes made of the Roman Catholic upbringing of both Hitler and Goebbels. In particular it is suggested that the National Socialist love of ceremony derived from the processions which Hitler had seen as a boy in Catholic churches. The great party days and rallies in Nuremberg and elsewhere are modern pieces of cinema more than they are overtly liturgical. It would probably be truer to say that the modern Roman Catholic Church, with its widely filmed papal coronations, its open-air masses in sports stadiums and its torch-lit processions through the streets of Lourdes, learnt from the National Socialists, rather than the other way about.

As well as the historians who lay emphasis on the Catholic upbringing, it was something to which Hitler himself often made allusion, and he was nearly always violently hostile. 'The biretta! The mere sight of these abortions in cassocks makes me wild!'[1] Hitler saw himself as having avoided the power of the priests. 'In Austria, religious instruction was given by the priests. I was the eternal asker of questions. Since I was completely the master of the material' – but naturally – 'I was unassailable.' Nevertheless, even as the unassailable war leader in January 1942, he would sit in the middle of the night and remember the power of a certain Father Schwarz at his first school. 'When Father Schwarz entered the classroom, the atmosphere was at once transformed. He brought revolution in with him. For my part, I used to excite him by waving pencils in the colours of the Greater Germany. "Put away those abominable colours at once!" he'd say … "You should have no other ideal in your heart but that of our beloved country and our beloved house of Habsburg. Whoever does not love the Imperial Family, does not love the Church, and whoever does not love the Church, does not love God! Sit down, Hitler!"[2] In that sentence, if you substitute the Leader for the emperor, and the party for Church, you have the template for the kind of obedience which would come to be expected of Germans under the National Socialist revolution.

What both Goebbels and Hitler did probably learn from their Catholic upbringing was a system of control. In the years when they were growing up, the Catholic Church throughout Europe had seen a catastrophic decline in numbers. Its leadership felt itself threatened by what was called Modernism, the attempt to reconcile scientific learning, modern Biblical scholarship and modern philosophy with the evolving teaching of Christianity. In 1906, the Pope, Pius X, had issued a savage attack on the Modernists and instituted what was in effect a purge of the Church. Catholics were encouraged to tell tales on any priest or religious figure who seemed to be tainted with Modernism. There were extraordinary cases of stray conversations overheard on railway journeys being reported to the authorities, and careers in the Church being ruined in consequence. The Church displayed what was in effect thought-policing. Its techniques were eagerly copied by the extremist politicians of Left and Right in subsequent generations.

When someone begged the Pope to have mercy on a suspected Modernist, Pius X replied, 'Kindness is for fools.' Hitler hated Catholicism and in time came to persecute it. But he learnt much from watching its system of power. He told Heinrich Himmler (who had been there from the time of the Munich putsch and who would become the chief implementer of the Final Solution, the massacre of Europe's Jews) and SS General Reinhard Heydrich one evening in 1941 how much he had admired, as a youth, the way in which the Pope and his henchmen had put down Modernism in 1905–6.[3] He admired the dedication of its celibate clergy. He admired, too, the fact that it was classless. 'A simple cowherd can become a cardinal. That's why the Church remains militant.'[4] He admired its unchanging teachings. He admired its ability to intrude and snoop into private lives. He admired its lack of kindness. Above all, he admired its organizational skills. Always and everywhere, Catholic parishes, schools and dioceses, academies, and youth groups, guaranteed that the faith was propagated in each area. And it was always the same faith, rigidly controlled by the bosses of the hierarchy. More, even, than the Communists, it was the Catholics who had control over the minds of their adherents. Hitler and Goebbels, the two Catholic renegades, recreated a political organization which was comparable to a Church, with its own youth movement, its own simple educational programme or catechism, its own thought police, even the equivalent of the Jesuit order in the elite paramilitary guard, the SS. So superbly well organized had the National Socialist Party become, in a Germany which was rapidly falling into chaos in all its government departments, that the Nazis created, well before they were actually rewarded with political power, a power-structure which had huge control over human lives.

A key component of this structure was the Hitler Youth organization (Hitler Jugend, or HJ). Here the side of Hitler which had admired the novels of Karl May, and who understood the young because he was in many respects childish, came into its own. National Socialism was a young movement. Its chief appeal was to the younger generation. The huge proportion of members of the SA were, naturally enough, young unemployed men. In the consolidation of Nazi power, it was necessary to start a specific youth movement, analogous to Baden Powell's Scout movement, to counteract the influence of comparable Communist youth movements. Every child who joined could enter a little into the Leader's own fantasy life and become a Red Indian brave like Karl May's Winnetou, or a lone-ranging cowboy like Old Surehand. Upon enrolment, the boy would be given a dagger on which the words 'Blood and Honour' were engraved. Unlike the more seemly Boy Scouts, the Hitler Youth also had an exciting lack of respectability. When he put on his uniform, the boy would be told that he was superior to a mere civilian. 'We took this to mean we could beat up civilians if they gave themselves airs', said one former HJ member.[5] Many German boys flocked to join the Hitler Youth, which gave them the chance, in hard economic times, to enjoy sport, and comradeship, and to sleep in tents. When the Nazis took power, the

Hitler Youth movement was one of the features of German life which most impressed foreign visitors. Apart from its levels of discipline, it so visibly increased not merely morale but physical health. This was at a time when the youth of English cities, for example, were undernourished, and suffering from rickets, tuberculosis and other diseases. Sir Arnold Wilson, an MP who visited Germany seven times during the period 1933–9, remarked, 'Infant mortality has been greatly reduced, tuberculosis and other diseases have noticeably diminished. The criminal courts have never had so little to do, and the prisons never had so few occupants. It is a pleasure to observe the physical aptitude of German youth.' Very many people, in Germany and outside, would have echoed these words from the time of the Hitler Youth movement's inception, and its popularity, among young people and among their parents, was a key factor in the Nazi electoral success of 1931–3.

In a pamphlet about the training of young people, a Nazi author wrote, 'For us an order and an imperative are the most sacred duties. For every order comes from the responsible personage and that personage we trust – the Leader. So we stand before you, the German Father, the German Mother, we the young leaders of the German Youth, we train and educate your son, and mould him into a man of action, a man of victory. He has been taken into a hard school so that his fists may be steeled, his courage strengthened, and that he may be given a faith, a faith in Germany.'[6]

Very many Germans, in the anarchy which characterized the last days of the Weimar Republic, felt that a faith in

Germany would not come amiss. One of the factors which allowed the Nazis eventually to take power was the fear of the army felt by the soft Left. They dreaded a military or quasi-military government, led by President Hindenburg's close adviser, the right-wing Major Kurt von Schleicher. He was one of the many 'useful idiots' who believed that he could use Hitler for his own purposes. Schleicher's politics were extreme nationalist. Of course, a military dictatorship under Schleicher would have been tough, but hindsight can be fairly sure it would have been mild compared with what actually came.

Schleicher patronizingly told Hindenburg that Hitler was 'an interesting man with exceptional speaking abilities. In his plans he outsoars the clouds. You then have to hold him by the coat-tails to keep him on the ground.'[7] It was a genuinely fatal judgement, since Hitler would have Schleicher executed on 30 June 1934.

In the chaos of elections and collapsing governments, Hindenburg, a failing, ancient figure from a now vanished Wilhelmine German past, appointed as Chancellor a Catholic aristocrat called Franz von Papen. Papen was even less equipped than Schleicher to deal with the demons being unleashed by the Nazi magic. But, like Schleicher, he also believed that he could manipulate the Nazis, do deals with them, 'use' them as a weapon against the Left. Being a man who was, however morally weak, basically sane, Papen could not even see the magic at work. As for Hitler, Papen said, 'I could detect no inner quality which might explain his extraordinary hold on the masses. He was wearing a dark

blue suit and seemed the complete petit bourgeois. He had an
unhealthy complexion and with his little moustache and
curious hairstyle had an indefinable bohemian quality. His
demeanour was modest and polite and although I heard
much about the magnetic quality of his eyes, I do not remember being impressed by him ...'[8]

The country meanwhile was in anarchy, with general elections being held on an almost monthly basis. In order to
secure the support of the Nazis, Schleicher was getting
Hindenburg to concede more and more privileges to them. A
major mistake was in lifting the ban on private armies, and
allowing the SS and the SA into the arena of domestic politics. By now, the Nazis had set in place their perfect formula
for revolutionary control of the country. They had established a nationwide organization, each with its own local
leaders, or Gauleiters (Gau is the word for an area or region).
They had established a popular youth movement, which, to
the relief of anxious, unemployed parents, kept their boys off
the streets, and kept them fit and active. They had also, with
increasing visibility, established the fact that they were frightening. There was now no town in Germany which did not
have its brown-shirted storm-troopers standing beside the
local Jewish shop, or Jewish dentist (most of the dentists in
Germany were Jewish) or doctor's surgery. It was beginning
to require courage to defy them. The majority of the leadership of the Lutheran Church were, if not openly sympathetic
to the Nazis, at least prepared to do a deal with them. Only a
few saw what an infernal chasm was opening up before

German feet. One of these, the admirable Dietrich Bonhoeffer, had spoken, even before Hitler took power, of the possibility that they would have to suffer martyrdom at the hands of the Nazis. He was one of the leaders of the breakaway anti-Nazi schism in the Lutheran Church – the so-called Confessing Church. Within weeks of Hitler's assumption of power he made a radio broadcast, which was cut off mid-sentence, in which he warned the German people against the cult of personality and said that the *Führer* would turn out to be the *Verführer* – the Leader would be a Seducer.

By August 1932, the Nazis were doing so well in the polls, and the mainstream or semi-sane parties were in such disarray, that Goebbels was urging Hitler to go for bust. They conveyed to Schleicher in secret talks that he should tell the President that Hitler would only consent to serve in a government if he could be the Chancellor of Germany. Schleicher initially thought he was joking. It was out of the question! Even Schleicher, who had in fact done so much to assist the Nazis' rise to power, could not see what was happening.

Not long afterwards, Papen proposed that maybe they should offer Hitler the post in what he called a Brown–Black (Nazi–Catholic) coalition. Papen clearly had no idea that such an idea was out of the question.

Hitler was a good hand at the political poker game. At the very beginning of his career he had managed to oust the pathetic founder-membership of Anton Drexler's Nazi Party, and to say, in effect, that unless he had total control, he would not play. The same technique worked with the hardened politicians of Germany's sane Right, and would later prove effective with the Prime Minister of Great Britain, then the greatest imperial world power. All or Nothing.

The Nothing, and this was the advancing dread of the German Right, was Communism. Papen was in many respects like the British Prime Minister Neville Chamberlain and his Foreign Secretary Lord Halifax, who felt that Mussolini in Italy was better than the Communists, and Hitler better than a Bolshevist German dictator.

In August, with Papen still holding on to the Chancellorship, they offered Hitler the post of Vice Chancellor. 'The idea of the Leader as Vice Chancellor in a bourgeois Cabinet is too grotesque to be taken seriously', was the view of Goebbels. Hitler emerged from this round of political talks with a feeling of abject defeat. He had not been given the Chancellorship, and it looked as if the government was going to limp on without the overt support of the 13 million or so Nazi activists in the country.

In the late summer and autumn, the Nazis kept up their pincer campaign of, on the one hand, political intrigue at the highest levels, and on the other, lowest level, street violence and murder. The violence turned public attention away from the humiliating fact that President Hindenburg had failed to make Hitler Chancellor. Papen brought in an emergency decree allowing a peremptory death sentence for acts of political, terrorist murder. Local SA leaders threatened mayhem, the smashing of Jewish shops, and the usual horrors, if death sentences were carried out against Nazis.

The Reichstag was dissolved in September and the fifth general election in one year was announced. In October, the Nazis staged a huge youth rally in Potsdam. There were by now grave doubts about party funding and money was tight. One of Hitler's earliest supporters, Kurt Lüdecke, a rich gambling playboy, came back from America with some much needed funds. Hitler, whose spirits were low, had been in some doubts about whether he would be able to rise to the occasion of the youth rally, to which 110,000 boys and girls were coming from all over Germany. But as Lüdecke later remembered: 'when Hitler stood alone at the front of the platform, a fantastic cry went up into the night, a sound of matchless jubilation. Then he raised his arms and dead silence fell. He burst into a flaming address which lasted scarcely fifteen minutes. Again he was the old Hitler, spontaneous, fiery, full of appeal.'[9] For seven hours, the Hitler Youth then paraded past him.

The November election led to another stalemate. The German electorate was more or less evenly divided, with a slight drop in the Nazi vote. Nevertheless, on 19 November, a petition was handed to Hindenburg, signed by twenty of the leaders of Germany's greatest businesses, demanding that Hitler be offered the Chancellorship. Hindenburg again offered Hitler a place in the coalition, and again Hitler refused. Schleicher replaced Papen as Chancellor.

Schleicher then delivered what could have been a killer blow to Hitler's movement. He offered a place in his government to Gregor Strasser, the inventor of the term 'the politics of catastrophe'. Strasser was a racist, a believer in thuggery, a Nazi. But he was a Nazi without Hitler's black poetry, a Nazi without the Wagner-mysticism or the personal magnetism. Hitler moved fast. With the help of Hess, he combed through the movement with the speed and efficiency of one of Pius X's *monsignori* spying out Modernists among the Catholic clergy in 1906. Any likely Strasser supporter was immediately removed from his position of influence or rank in the party. Strasser himself became isolated and such were the scare-tactics employed by the Nazi majority that his support ebbed away. He, in the end, funked accepting Schleicher's offer of a job in government. 'Strasser is isolated! Dead man!' noted Goebbels gleefully.

The crisis had demonstrated Hitler's enormous personal power in the party. It was a case of *L'état c'est moi*. It was no longer possible for any right-wing government to think of harnessing Nazi support without involving Hitler. And Hitler refused to be part of any government of which he was not the leader.

In January 1933, with the government lurching towards yet more political and economic crises, Papen foolishly believed that he saw a way of ousting Schleicher from the Chancellorship. He began cosying up to Hitler. Local elections in Lippe-Detmold that January showed a surge of Nazi support. With the withdrawal of support by the Centre Left and by Papen, Schleicher had no alternative but to recommend to the President yet another election, since the government could not hope to survive a vote of no confidence in the Reichstag.

By the end of January, Papen was recommending that Hindenburg appoint Hitler as Chancellor on condition that he had a Cabinet of conservatives.

Hitler's state of nervous agitation as these negotiations were in progress had reached a state of near-delirium. 'I have never seen him in such a state', said Joachim von Ribbentrop, who was destined to be Nazi Germany's fatally influential foreign minister.

Hitler wanted power so badly that it had driven him to frenzy. The Nazis would always speak of their victory as if it were a Rienzi-style act of political energy and violence – *Die Machtergreifung*, the seizure of power. In fact, Hitler became the Chancellor of Germany just as many others have done since in milder and more democratic times, by a series of telephone calls and a succession of compromises. Papen believed that he had neutered Hitler – he was 'no danger at all. We've hired him for our act!' – by insisting that all but two of the seats in the Cabinet be occupied by conservatives, not Nazis. Hitler played the much stronger card, while agreeing to this, of insisting that they all consent to an 'Enabling Act' which would be brought into force as soon as he had taken office. The Enabling Act would grant him Emergency Powers. These would, of course, as anyone could surely have foretold, entail the abolition of democracy in Germany and the handing to Adolf Hitler of more or less absolute power.

Papen consented. On 30 January, General Hindenburg, the President of Germany, agreed that the Chancellorship be given to Adolf Hitler. When Hitler received the news, he immediately alerted the Berlin Brownshirts to go onto the streets. The new Cabinet called on the President. Hindenburg appeared to be in a daze. Hitler, *endimanché* in a black frock coat and clutching a top hat, told 'the old man' that he would serve him as loyally as he had done when he was a soldier in the war. It was not usual for speeches to be made on these occasions and everyone looked embarrassed and shifty. Hindenburg was so disconcerted that he never in fact went through the formula of offering Hitler the Chancellorship. He merely said gruffly, 'And now, gentlemen, forward with God!'

Hitler's first act was to assemble the Cabinet and tell them that the Reichstag would be dissolved and new elections held to grant him the emergency powers necessary to deal with the crisis. As darkness fell over Berlin, the Stahlhelm units (who in the old Freikorps days had been a rival right-wing group) joined forces with the SA and 25,000 men marched in a torch-lit procession through the Brandenburg Gate and past the Chancellery. In the light of what followed, it is the pious custom of historians to emphasize with what chill all decent people greeted this spectacle. The truth is that the Nazis were extremely popular, and that Hitler, all of whose views and plans had been repeatedly yelled through loud-hailers and microphones to the multitudes, was seen as just what Germany needed. Over 50,000 Berliners joined the Nazi Party in the month after his accession to power.[10]

SIX

1933–1936 Old Surehand

Henry Williamson, the author of the charming and popular story *Tarka the Otter*, described Adolf Hitler in 1936 as 'the great man across the Rhine whose symbol is a happy child'. Two days after Hitler's appointment as Chancellor, General Ludendorff, who had stood at Hitler's side in the 1923 Munich putsch and who had now seen what sort of a man he was, wrote to President Hindenburg, 'I solemnly prophesy to you that this damnable man will plunge our Reich into the abyss and bring inconceivable misery down upon our nation. Coming generations will curse you in your grave because of this action.'[1]

It would seem obvious to us, with the eyes of hindsight, that Williamson was a deluded fool and that Ludendorff spoke as he knew. Why could the majority of Germans not see – when the new regime immediately set up its hateful Secret State Police (Geheime Staatspolizei), the Gestapo, when snoopers began to insist upon a census into every German citizen's private life, racial background and religion? Why did the huge majority of Germans not see that a terrible mistake had been made, when the nation of Europeans who had given to the world the invention of the printed book instituted that chilling re-enactment of the Inquisition: the burning of books? What possessed Ernst Bertram, a literate man, to compose a lyric to be sung as the books were heaped up in funeral pyres of culture:

> Reject what confuses you
> Outlaw what seduces you,
> What did not spring from a pure will,
> Into the flames with what threatens you!

This was to celebrate the burning of, among other books, the work of his friend Thomas Mann, the lyrics of Heinrich Heine, and many other ornaments of German greatness. How could they have felt happy at such things? Admittedly, not all did – 250 noted writers and academics left the country as soon as Hitler became Chancellor.

The White Queen in *Through the Looking Glass* remarked that it is a poor sort of memory which only works backwards. Without an understanding of this truth, the study of history is impossible. Perspectives change with time. Most people are not capable of seeing into the future. Hindsight allows us to see things which were invisible to them. And to us these things seem so blindingly obvious that we wonder: how could they have been so blind?

When we consider the period in Germany, let us say, from Hitler becoming Chancellor in January 1933 to the splendid pageantry of the Olympic Games in 1936, it is particularly necessary to attempt an act of stupendous historical imagination: to think of Hitler and the National Socialist revolution without any knowledge of where it led in the years which followed 1936. Naturally, there were those who, for a variety of reasons, found the Nazis, and Hitler, repellent, all through these years of apparent triumph. The systematic anti-Semitism of the regime was alone enough to excite the contempt of decent people. If anyone had foretold, in January 1933, that the Nazis would be able to massacre about 6 million Jews, many of them being gassed in specially constructed death camps, their prophecy would have been dismissed as fantasy. The anti-Semitism in which German people, and the rest of the world, colluded in these early days was a much more low-key affair. We can see that it ended in the trains, carrying millions of people to their deaths, and the scar of this everlastingly horrible memory is branded on European consciousness, as is the memory of the war, instigated by Hitler in 1939 and which led to perhaps 50 million deaths.

The majority of the Jews who died in this ghastly mass slaughter were not, of course, German citizens. When the Nazis took control statisticians reported that fewer than 1 per cent of German citizens were religious Jews (approximately 525,000 people) with a rather larger number of 'Jewish Germans of mixed race' – some 750,000.[2] In the last election before his appointment as Chancellor, Hitler had not stressed his anti-Semitic obsessions, and in the first year of his government, the Nazis moved slowly. On 7 April 1933, they passed a law which made it possible to purge Jews and others from the civil service. This included a wide range of callings, from judges to policemen to village schoolmasters.

Julius Streicher, whose rabidly anti-Jewish speeches and publications had enlivened public meetings for more than a decade, was put in charge of the central committee of the Nazi Party and on 1 April 1933, he called for a boycott on all Jewish businesses, shops, doctors, lawyers and dentists. For days beforehand, the SA were at work, daubing crudely painted signs outside shop doorways with the word JEW, and on the day of the boycott, SA heavies, some of them armed, stood at the doorways of shops, asking customers to withhold their patronage. In those early days, there were brave men such as Edwin Landau, a shopkeeper in a small west Prussian town, who donned his war medals and went to confront the bullies standing at the doors of other Jewish shops. Professor Viktor Klemperer, whose extensive diaries of the Nazi regime are essential reading, was forced to stand down as a professor of romance languages at Dresden University, but he noted in his diary on 25 April 1933 that he did not consider the German people to be especially anti-Semitic.

The maltreatment of Jews, and the beatings, and the monstrous beginnings of legislation against them gave sufficient warning signals to many that they were no longer safe in Germany. But there were those such as Peter Gay and his family in Berlin who felt that the dictatorship was sending mixed messages, and that it was 'safe enough for them to remain'.[3]

The blindness of people to Nazi intentions – or, if not of a full-scale programme of extermination at this date, then at least to Nazi predilections – can perhaps be attributed to two causes. First is the enormous sense of relief which flooded over Germany at the end of the ineffectual Weimar Republic. And the second is what were perceived as miraculous social and economic improvements by the regime.

The relief was expressed by otherwise highly intelligent human beings. Gerhart Hauptmann, a Nobel prize winner, published an article entitled 'I Say Yes!' Its sentiments were those of millions of Germans who were prepared to overlook the obvious brutality of the Brownshirts and the hideousness of anti-Semitic rhetoric from Goebbels and Streicher, because they felt that something had happened to their country. It seemed possible to put an end to the humiliation. 'A Pledge of Loyalty by German Writers to the People's Chancellor Adolf Hitler' was voluntarily signed by distinguished names, among them Martin Heidegger – one of the most revered philosophers of the twentieth century. Heidegger's inaugural lecture at the University of Freiburg was a paean of praise to the Leader, and the podium from which he spoke was festooned with the red banners and swastikas of the movement. Richard Strauss, by any standards one of the best composers of the twentieth century, placed himself at the regime's disposal. Gottfried Benn, the poet, wrote to the exiled Klaus Mann – 'On purely personal grounds I declare myself for the new State, because it is my Volk that is making its way now. Who am I to exclude myself; do I know anything better? No! ... My intellectual and economic existence, my language, my life, my human relationships, the entire sum of my brain, I owe primarily to this Volk. My ancestors came from it; my children return to it ...'[4]

Such were the feelings of unbounded relief which the National Socialist victory occasioned in the minds of many people who were not in themselves sinister, and who meant no harm to others. But they would have been peculiar indeed had they not been sustained by the apparent success of the social and economic programme which Adolf Hitler initiated from the moment of taking office. Klemperer, no friend to the regime, bumped into a stranger in a busy street in Dresden on 24 November 1936. 'A young man hurries past me in the crowd, a complete stranger, half turns and says with a beaming face, "I've got work – the first time in three years – and good work – at Renner's – they pay well! – for four weeks! –" and runs on.'[5]

Someone who was friendly towards the regime remarked on the tendency of historians to identify the tyrannies of Stalin and Hitler. 'But in Stalin's Russia, the great majority were visibly unhappy. You have only to read Nadezhda Mandelstam's memoirs to see how unhappy they were. In Germany in the early years of the regime, you could *feel, see*, the happiness.'[6] The historian Robert Gellately wrote in 2001 that 'Hitler won acclaim in the 1930s, perhaps first and foremost for beating the Great Depression, and for curing the massive unemployment in the country. Although definitely no economist himself, his regime overcame the Depression more quickly than any of the other advanced industrial nations.'[7]

This is an absolutely fundamental fact to grasp. Without it, very little else about the Third Reich is comprehensible. It was by no means only Fascists, such as Henry Williamson, who felt happy that Hitler was now the supreme Leader. Lord Rothermere, proprietor of the *Daily Mail*, and Ward Price, the editor of that popular English newspaper, dined with Hitler in December 1933. Hitler, who wore full evening dress, rather than uniform, withdrew at the end of the meal to a room reserved for non-smokers, and Rothermere joined him. He was deeply impressed and the *Daily Mail* became a broadly pro-Hitler newspaper for several years thereafter.[8] When Hitler went to breakfast at the British embassy in Berlin in March 1935 together with Göring and Ribbentrop, Sir Eric Phipps, the ambassador, had lined up his children in the reception room to raise their little arms and exclaim a bashful 'Heil Hitler!'[9] When supping at the Chancellery a few months later with Winifred Wagner, wearing the simple brown shirt of an SA officer, Hitler slapped his thigh and exclaimed, 'Great people, the English!'[10]

Monsignor Ludwig Kaas, the leader of the recently outlawed Catholic Party, felt able to tell the Pope, Pius XI, that 'Hitler knows how to guide the ship ... Even before he became Chancellor, I met him frequently and was greatly impressed by his clear thinking, by his way of facing realities while upholding his ideals, which are noble.' And the Pope, an amiable scholar and former Vatican librarian, was delighted, on 20 July 1933, to sign a concordat with the Third Reich. When he did so, His Holiness met Hitler's representative, Papen, 'most graciously and remarked how pleased he was that the German Government now had at its head a man uncompromisingly opposed to Communism and Russian nihilism in all its forms.'[11]

The dread of Communism extending its tentacles across the whole of Europe blinded all these people to the reality of what Hitler was actually like. The Catholic leaders, for example, could not know that Hitler was fanatically anti-Catholic or that he would eventually imprison over 20,000 priests in Dachau. They could know, by now, that he was a rabid anti-Semite, but this did not trouble them. For them, as for the proprietor of the *Daily Mail*, Hitler was their strongest ally against Communism.

At that date they were probably right. And now that we know the full extent of Stalin's gulags, the sheer terribleness of a system which required so high a proportion of its population to be enslaved or imprisoned, we might conclude, even with hindsight, that they were right. Hitler *was* a bulwark against Stalinism. For this reason, there were many who were prepared to overlook the rough justice with which he treated Reds or potential subversives.

Within a month of Hitler becoming Chancellor, the Communists had planned demonstrations, armed resistance and arson. Then, on 27 February, a young Dutchman named Marinus van der Lubbe, having failed in his attempt to set fire to three government buildings, crept into the Reichstag and set fire to it with four packets of firelighters.[12] It was an isolated incident by a fanatic but it was easy, as the flames soared into the night sky of Berlin, for Hitler and his Nazi colleagues in the government to see it as a Communist plot. In private, Hitler's first reaction to the fire in the parliament building was to say, 'Good riddance to that trashy old shack!' He had no more interest in preserving parliamentary debate than did the Communists. But in public he was able to say that if the Communists had power in Europe it would only be a matter of months before the whole continent was aflame like that building.

He could use the fire as an excuse to declare a state of national emergency and to use truckloads of SA auxiliaries to help the police maintain 'order'. 'When the Communist menace is stamped out the normal order of things shall return. Our laws are too liberal for us to deal effectively with this Bolshevist underworld.'

The following day, on 28 February, Hitler suspended all press freedom, as well as freedom of assembly and expression. Henceforward, even to make the mildest joke about the Leader could result in a midnight knock on the door from the Gestapo. Conservatives, both of the capitalist industrialist type and of the older officers in the military, were perfectly happy for democracy to be suspended. Such figures as Gustav Krupp von Bohlen pledged a million marks for the Ruhr combine. I. G. Farben gave 400,000 marks to help revive the industrial plants there.

The use of the Brownshirts to maintain order was, however, not something which the old-fashioned military were prepared to tolerate. Hindenburg and the other senior military made it clear to Hitler that he could not have a private army within the Reich. From now on, the German army was prepared to pledge him their personal support on condition that he drastically limited the street-powers of the SA.

Hitler knew that he could not remain in power without the support of the regular German army and its officers. He therefore made the decision to liquidate his old friend Röhm, who was in any case now openly hostile to Hitler himself, and to what he regarded as the sell-out to respectability which taking government had entailed. Göring, Goebbels, Himmler and the rest of the pack were settling down to positions of real political power. Röhm wanted to continue the revolution. He wanted to put the 'socialist' back into National Socialist. His 'sacred socialism seeking the whole'[13] would be achieved – for Röhm if not for the movement as a whole – by active homosexuality with street boys and maintaining an implacable distrust of the industrialists such as Krupp who were financing and entrenching Hitler's position in the German industrial heartlands. 'Adolf is rotten', Röhm complained. 'He's betraying all of us. He only goes around with reactionaries. His old comrades aren't good enough for him.'

Röhm had an insight into Hitler's character which was basically true: 'Adolf was and always will be a civilian, an "artist", a dreamer … Right now all he wants to do is sit up in the mountains and play God. And guys like us have to cool our heels ... He wants to inherit a ready-made army all set to go.'[14]

This was all absolutely true. Hitler had bursts of energy and activity, spells of rage-fuelled hyper-activity, but for the most part he was, unlike Röhm, extremely lazy; he was a dreamer, and he was always more of an artist than a soldier. He did indeed see the value of inheriting ready-made institutions and using them for his own purposes. Even during the years before he came to power, when we might expect the party leader to have been busily occupied with gaining political ground, his way of life was that of the lazy bohemian. He never kept regular hours, and he was seldom seen to do any work in his large work room at the Berghof. Afternoons were invariably spent, during those days, at the Café Heck or some similar place, surrounded by admirers, and talking.

By the time he became Chancellor, the pattern of life did not markedly change. He rose late, spent most of the day chatting, and would nearly always round off the evening with a film. Adjutants tried to find him a new film to watch every day. His earlier fondness for high culture began to diminish. He enjoyed 'light entertainment', and if women, such as his girlfriend Eva Braun, were present in the evenings, political conversation was banned – as was, of course, that cardinal sin, smoking.

To say that he was an artist and a civilian was not to deny that his political aims were belligerent. But he did not plan to accomplish them by means of Röhm and his street Arabs.

The SA was useful to bully Jews and frighten the Reds, but for the bigger plan – as yet not fully disclosed to the German people – namely the expansion by force into Eastern Europe – the German army was an absolute necessity. It was the generals, whom Röhm dismissed as old fogies, who would enable Hitler to become the new Napoleon, and not the Brownshirts.

So Röhm had to go. And as for National Socialist doctrine – beyond the broad outlines of a plan for an absolutist, anti-Semitic state with the ambition to expand east and west throughout Europe – Hitler was actually untroubled by the details which appealed so strongly to the core party enthusiasts.

The so-called Night of the Long Knives, 30 June 1934, not only saw the murder of Röhm and other influential SA officers. It was the excuse to polish off such miscellaneous figures as the former Chancellor, General Schleicher, and his wife, gunned down in their house, Gregor Strasser (taken to Gestapo headquarters and shot), the head of Catholic Action, Erich Klausener, and other political figures who might be thought to have stood in the Leader's way. In a two-hour-long speech in the Reichstag, Hitler justified the killings – 'Mutinies are broken according to eternal iron laws.' Although thirteen members of the parliament had died in the purge, no one rose to protest at this method of justice. Probably as many as 200 people had been gunned down in one night without trial. The Nazis drafted a telegram which they made Hindenburg send to the Leader: FROM THE REPORTS PLACED BEFORE ME I

LEARN THAT BY YOUR DETERMINED ACTION AND GALLANT
PERSONAL INTERVENTION YOU HAVE NIPPED TREASON IN THE
BUD. YOU HAVE SAVED THE GERMAN NATION FROM SERIOUS
DANGER. FOR THIS I EXPRESS TO YOU MY MOST PROFOUND
THANKS AND SINCERE APPRECIATION.

The extermination of Röhm and the downgrading of the
SA had come about as a result of detailed negotiations with
the army. In April 1934 Hitler had secretly met the War
Minister, General Werner von Blomberg, on board the battle-
ship *Deutschland*. They had agreed that the army would
support Hitler becoming President, as well as Chancellor, on
Hindenburg's death. The quid pro quo was the elimination of
Röhm, and the day after that happened, Blomberg issued an
order of the day to the troops commending the Leader's
'soldierly' decision. On 2 August, Hindenburg died, and Hitler,
with the full support of the army, now assumed the Presidency.
It was agreed that rather than being called Chancellor or
President he would in future simply be known as The Leader.
This was put to a plebiscite on 19 August and 89.9 per cent of
German people voted 'Yes'. Blomberg remained in office until
January 1938 when an embarrassing scandal forced him to
resign. Hitler and Göring were witnesses at his wedding to a
much younger bride, Margarethe Gruhn, who had, it tran-
spired, been posing for pornographic pictures for a Jewish
Czech photographer who was also her lover. Her name also
appeared on the police register of Berlin prostitutes.

Hitler did not replace Blomberg. He merely took over the
total domination of the armed forces. He was assisted in the

administrative task of being Commander in Chief by his devotee General Wilhelm Keitel, who testified at Nuremberg: 'From then on, Hitler gave orders directly to the army, the navy and the air force. No one issued orders independently of Hitler.'[15]

All this lay a little in the future. Before the years of militaristic triumph, there were the years of a seemingly miraculous economic recovery. Gone were the strikes. Gone were the unemployment queues. The miracle had been accomplished by vast schemes of public works, the building of the motorways (autobahns), the improvement of the nation's infrastructure, and by putting Germany on a war economy (surreptitiously manufacturing parts for aircraft and tanks) while superficially celebrating the prosperity of peace. John Maynard Keynes was vainly urging the democratic governments of Europe to 'prime the pump' and inject money artificially into their flagging economies. Hitler, like President Roosevelt in America, put Keynesianism into action. In Roosevelt's case, it was Keynes with 'fireside chats' delivered by radio to the grateful recipients of his 'New Deal'. With Hitler, it was Keynes set to a lurid Wagnerian music.

The economic recovery was played out against a repeated programme of public spectacles. Hitler the architect and stage-designer, Hitler the would-be operatic impresario, made the story of Germany's recovery into a vulgar pageant of forward-looking nationalism. At Nuremberg, he staged rallies which were breathtakingly spectacular. He engaged the services of a young architect named Albert Speer, who erected a twentieth-century equivalent of pagan games in the world of ancient Sparta or Pergamum. It was in fact the altars of Pergamum which were the inspiration for Speer's huge tribune structure in the stadium at Nuremberg, which was eighty feet high and crowned by an eagle with a wing-span of 100 feet. At 40-feet intervals were anti-aircraft searchlights with a range of 25,000 feet. At the 1934 *Parteitag* – Party Day – over 200,000 National Socialists marched into the stadium's Zeppelin Field, with 20,000 unfurled banners, with lights, with torches, and, as a symbol of their return both to work and to military strength, tools of toil and weapons of war held aloft. Never in the history of the world had there been political displays on quite this scale. The effects on the huge crowds of the special lighting, of the punctiliously choreographed marches and gymnastic displays, of the songs and the lights were ecstatically excit-ing. Others in the world watched, and sought to imitate, the effect. For example, when the old librarian of the Vatican, Pius XI, died and was replaced by a former Papal Nuncio to Berlin, Eugenio Pacelli, he was crowned with a greater public display, and with more outdoor special effects, than had ever been used before by a Pope. It was directly inspired by the Nuremberg rallies, as were the great march-pasts of tanks and weaponry on Red Square which became a regular feature of life in the Soviet Union. Sir Eric Phipps's succes-sor as British ambassador to Berlin was overwhelmed by the Nazi pageantry. He recalled, 'I spent six years in St Petersburg before the war in the best days of the old Russian ballet, but for grandiose beauty I have never seen a ballet to compare with it.'[16]

Speer, of all those close to Hitler, is in some ways the most depressing, since he was a 'normal' man, cold-heartedly cynical and with no particular political beliefs. Another figure who prostituted superb talent to glorify the regime was Leni Riefenstahl, who had made her name with the film *The Blue Light*, and now recorded the 1934 Party Day as an unforgettable cinematic spectacle – *Triumph of the Will*. From its opening sequences, in which Hitler is, back-view, in an aeroplane descending upon Nuremberg, Riefenstahl made him into a parody of Christ returning to earth, or at the very least a Lohengrin coming on his swan to save his people. Riefenstahl was a film-maker of enormous talent, with a very sure eye. People gossiped, as they did about Winifred Wagner, about the extent of her intimacy with the Leader. In a rather nauseating anecdote, she afterwards claimed that she had propositioned Hitler and that his reply was that he had given himself to Germany as to a lover. Somehow, the repetition of this story by one of the supposed participants is equally repellent, whether it is true or false.

It was not the Nazis alone, nor the Germans alone, who were manipulated into support of the regime by these vulgarized balletic scenes. In 1936, as it happened, the Olympic Games were scheduled to be held in Berlin. Three years would have passed, by the time the Games took place, from the time the Nazis came to power. They were three years in which the world had become electrified by the spectacle of Hitler's successes. On the one hand there were those who saw his transformation of the German economy and his routing of the Communists as signs of great hope. On the other side were those who could not believe that the belligerence of his speeches, and the obvious militarism of the regime, could foreshadow a peaceful future in Europe. Quite apart from Germany's aspiration to be reunited to Austria, or to occupy the German-speaking regions of Czechoslovakia and Poland, what of France? As Hitler spoke of revenge for the Treaty of Versailles, how was Germany's old enemy going to react? And apart from these territorial questions, the whole political division between the extremes of Left and Right appeared to have divided Europe – in Spain, in Italy, in Portugal. However terrible the millions of deaths in Soviet Russia, was it truly the case that the only alternative to the tyrannies of Communism were the brutalities of the Fascists?

It was against the background of these questions that the 1936 Olympic Games were held in Berlin. Those who attended them were by now fully acquainted with the fact that anti-Semitism was written into the Nazi view of the world. In 1935, the German Government had enacted the Nuremberg Laws – 'A Law for the Protection of German Blood and Honour'. This forebade 'Aryans' – to use the crazy classification of Houston Stewart Chamberlain – to marry or have children with 'non-Aryans'. There were restrictions even upon Jews employing non-Jewish servants and vice-versa. Having made it illegal for Jews to enjoy any close relations or intercourse with other Germans, and deprived them of the right to be policemen, teachers, lawyers, and so forth, it was hoped, as a British Foreign Office document of 1938 made clear, that the Jews would leave Germany peaceably. 'The ultimate aim of Germany's Jewish Policy is the emigration of all Jews living on German territories.' This was written at a time when only about 100,000 Jews had left Germany. As far as the author of the memorandum was concerned, the 'problem' here was not that Germany was persecuting the Jews, but that other nations would have to accept the exiles as refugees. Already, in readiness against this undesired eventuality, America, France, the Netherlands and Norway had legislation in place to restrict the numbers of Jews entering their countries.[17]

Incredible as it may seem to us in the post-Auschwitz world, most diplomatic and political experts throughout the world saw the Nuremberg legislations as 'moderate'. Instead of the bullying of the SA in the old days, the Germans were merely bringing in laws which restricted Jewish rights. It was only like Bismarck's *Kulturkampf* against the Catholics. If a nation wished to restrict membership of its civil service to Lutherans, why not?

Those who took this view were only too happy to turn a blind eye to its obvious monstrousness. And it was to appease these would-be friends of Germany that Hitler gave orders, in the run-up to the 1936 Olympics, that the cruder manifestations of anti-Semitism be played down or actually hidden. Gone were the signs telling Germans not to patronize Jewish shops or businesses. The Nazi propaganda sheets, and the speeches of the anti-Jewish rabble-rousers, were deliberately toned down. There was even a sense in Germany itself that perhaps the anti-Jewish stuff had simply been froth on top of the National Socialist beer. In the period 1934–8, even the rate of Jewish emigration slowed.[18]

The Olympic Games were a joint attempt, not just by the Germans, but by the human race, to turn a blind eye to what hindsight makes obvious: the essentially warlike, and essentially murderous, nature of Hitler's programme. Apart from the Leader refusing to shake hands with Jesse Owens, a black man from the United States who won four gold medals for athletics, the Olympics were a display in which the world apparently needed to be bamboozled. Richard Strauss arranged settings of the 'Horst-Wessel-Lied' and of 'Deutschland Über Alles' for a chorus of 3,000. A crowd of 100,000 cheered as Hitler took his place in the stand. All 250 of the French athletes enthusiastically gave him the Roman salute as they marched past his imperial stand. By the time the Games ended, the hypnotic effect of crowd-mania – upon which the Nazis had been playing so successfully for years at home – gripped the international crowd. When the Games ended on 16 August 1936, it was not only Germans who cried out, '*Sieg Heil! Unser Führer, Adolf Hitler! Sieg Heil!*'[19]

Diana Mitford, the most beautiful and intelligent of the celebrated aristocratic sisters, by now made regular visits to Berlin to see the Leader. Hitler, like many revolutionaries, was inordinately impressed by the very things he professed to despise. He was in awe of the fact that Diana's grandfather, the first Lord Redesdale, had translated the ur-Fascist text,

Houston Stewart Chamberlain's *Foundations of the Nineteenth Century*, into English. At Wagner's grave, he once said to Diana, 'I am unworthy to stand here. But *you* are worthy, because your grandfather was one of the great early Wagnerians.' She was a dazzlingly attractive personality, as well as a beauty, and it was no wonder that he was in awe of her – not least because he believed that as an aristocrat, and a cousin of Churchill's, she was close to the heart of the political world. 'Lady Mitford' – as he believed she was called – 'and her sisters are very much in the know, thanks to their relationship with influential people', he once told a group of friends.[20] He seemed to imagine that she was 'in the know' about military as well as social matters, and took it very seriously when she told him airily that she did not suppose there were more than three anti-aircraft guns in the whole of London. It was absurd to imagine that this vague, delightful woman would have known one end of an anti-aircraft gun from another: his taking her word on such a matter suggested a weakness on Hitler's part for upper class beauties.

She would stay at the Hotel Adlon and wait for the telephone in her bedroom to ring. When it did so, a voice, sometimes that of the Leader himself, but more usually an underling, would say, 'Gracious Lady, the Leader can see you now.' She would cross the Unter den Linden to the Chancellery and pass the evening in conversation with this remarkable man. If he was in a good humour, he could be funny, imitating Mussolini's strutting style, or – in high camp mode – pretending to be one of the women who doted upon him. Or they would discuss the music dramas of Wagner, or the international situation. A theme to which he returned over and over again was the miraculous bloodlessness of the Nazi revolution. To establish the Soviet system had taken a civil war in which millions of Russians had died. The Nazi revolution had taken place with only a few hundred dead.

Presumably, when Hitler spoke of a bloodless revolution, he was not thinking of those killed in the organized riots in the months following the fire in the Reichstag in 1933, those beaten up for attending concerts conducted by Fritz Busch, for example, who was dragged off his podium by Brownshirts because he was a Jew. He was forgetting the 500–600 probably killed in those months when the Mayor of Düsseldorf was attacked with a whip by a Nazi, when Jewish shops were plundered, and when, apart from those killed, some 100,000 troublemakers – Communists, liberals, Christians – were bundled off to concentration camps. He was also, of course, overlooking the murder of Röhm and friends, and the elimination of political rivals. Diana Mitford, and all the others who rejoiced in the triumph of Nazism, wanted, with at least part of themselves, to overlook the essential violence of the Nazi idea. The world wanted to overlook it, which is why the world, who by now had had time to read *My Struggle*, with its suggestion that the First World War would have been avoided if 12–15,000 Jews had been gassed, was very happy to turn up and enjoy the Olympic Games in Berlin.

Was not modern Germany a model of everything which the men and women in the stadium wanted for their own country? While 3 million Englishmen languished on the dole, and many more lived in poverty, Adolf Hitler had demonstrated that it was possible to create full employment. More than 1.5 million Germans were employed in the motor industry alone. All over Germany, there was now a modern road system – the autobahns. There was a sense, lacking in the democratic countries, that Hitler had given a whole country the capacity to be itself. Energy had returned. As the Nazi Woman's Movement, presided over by 'Reich Mother-in-Chief' Gertrud Scholtz-Klink, put it – in a slogan which perhaps seemed more inspirited at the time than it does after eighty years – 'The German Woman is Knitting Again!'[21]

SEVEN

1936–1939 The Road to War

In January 1936, Hitler summoned all his Gauleiters and Reichsleiters to a meeting. Disputes had arisen among them. There was disgruntlement among the old Brownshirt ranks that National Socialism had caved in to the establishment. As Hitler turned his eyes abroad and began to think about ways of realizing his nationalist dreams, the last thing he wanted was any disunity among the party faithful. His speech that January was full of emotion, ending with the promise that if they did not give him what he wanted, he would commit suicide. The ever-faithful Hess, when Hitler's extraordinary stream of self-pitying words came to a conclusion, assured the Leader that they would follow him wherever he led.

What Hitler had demanded was that the party leadership should be reorganized into a single entity, with himself as the absolute leader. He would likewise ask the leaders of the armed forces to make him their supreme war leader. The successes of the first three years in power had given him a hunger for absolute power which was inexhaustible.

He cheered up the Gauleiters and Reichsleiters by telling them that his plans for expansion could now begin. On 7 March three German battalions occupied the demilitarized Rhineland zone, that is all territory west of the Rhine and a thirty-mile strip east of the river taking in Cologne, Düsseldorf and Bonn. Far from being met by French tanks, as was feared, they were greeted by cheering crowds. Priests waving thuribles escorted the troops into their citadels.

It had been a bold gamble on Hitler's part. At this stage, Hitler had spoken a lot about rearmament but he was not yet in a position to fight a war with France. If the French chose to retaliate, Germany would have been forced into the humiliation of admitting that they were not ready for war. The British Foreign Secretary, Anthony Eden, expressed 'regret' over the move. The French did not act. Hitler had called their bluff.

In his domestic policy, Hitler had achieved what he claimed to have been a 'bloodless revolution'. It had certainly been a good deal less bloody than the French or the Russian revolutions, even if the end result was a police state in which Thomas Mann's novels were publicly burned, neighbours were encouraged to snoop upon one another and report suspected Jews or Communists to the secret police, and more and more absolute power was being handed to the leadership of one mentally unbalanced fanatic.

The stage was now set for a period of European history in which Hitler would attempt to apply the same good luck to foreign policy. Having brought about a Nazi revolution with the loss of only a few hundred lives, he would proceed, as he hoped, to conquer Europe by means of bluff, threat, histrionic speeches and big military displays.

Historians, economists and students of Hitler's remarkable personality debate a number of issues. One is whether the success of his economic and political revolution at home had, from the very beginning, depended upon putting Germany on a war economy – whether the economic miracle would have been possible if he had not all along been planning the war which would take millions of lives.

That is one issue. Another is whether hindsight shows us that war could have been avoided. If, at any one stage of his diplomatic master-strokes, he had been told that Britain, France and their allies would not allow what Hitler demanded, would he have retreated? Could peace in fact have been maintained had the Western Allies been braver in their resistance to Hitler?

A third question, which is of more immediate interest to his biographers, is the state of Hitler's health, and in particular of his mental health. By 1938, Sir Nevile Henderson, the British Ambassador in Germany, was expressing the view that the Leader was 'on the borderline of madness'.[1]

The answers to the first two sets of questions are, in the popular sense, academic, since all that matters is not what could have happened, but what did in fact happen. Hitler did, against the advice of his generals, deliberately advance Germany to a full-scale war footing by the end of the 1930s through military conscription and a covert programme of rearmament. The exact point at which he chose to do so, and whether he did so as a result of a long-hatched plan, as written about in *My Struggle*, or whether he did so inch by inch, scarcely aware of what he was doing, is irrelevant. So, too, is it irrelevant to ask whether peace could have been preserved if the British or the French had not followed the policy known as appeasement, allowing Hitler to dismantle Czechoslovakia in 1938–9. Events unfolded as they did. To ask whether things could have happened otherwise is the task not of history but of the parlour game.

Whether Hitler's medical condition affected events is, however, of direct relevance. Here the biographer must make a judgement. In 1944, only six years after Ambassador Henderson expressed the view that Hitler was mad, there was a famous plot to assassinate Hitler. It included many of the military top brass, and was supported by the brilliant young theologian Dietrich Bonhoeffer. The pastor's father, Dr Karl Bonhoeffer, the psychiatric director of Berlin's Charity Hospital, favoured a medical putsch, in which a team of doctors simply declared the Leader to be insane.

The medical profession is constantly revising what is, and is not, sanity, but there would surely be a case for suggesting that Hitler was at the very least mentally unbalanced, and that the imbalance from 1936 onwards became ever more pronounced, the temper-tantrums more extreme, the self-aggrandizement and self-pity taken to ever more operatic heights. And there is no doubt that Hitler's rages and excessive demands were so intolerable to those who came into his presence that they were prepared to do anything to appease them. How far he manipulated his 'madness' to achieve his political ends it is difficult to say.

From now onwards in his life, Hitler's medical history must be read alongside that of his political and military triumphs and disasters. His mother, Klara, had died just before Christmas 1907 aged only forty-seven. It was a death which obsessed him. Christmas was nearly always a gloomy time for him as he contemplated it.

When Hitler himself turned forty-seven, his health obsessions, which had always been acute, rose to levels of hypochondriacal paranoia. It is a paradoxical fact about human beings that they agonize about trivia and then make the big decisions on impulse – when choosing a wife or a house to live in. One would have expected so health-conscious an individual as Hitler to select a doctor of high reputation, perhaps from one of the best teaching hospitals in Berlin. But an essential ingredient in Hitler's nature was the con man's fear of being found out. When discussing military matters, he instinctively disliked the company of nearly all his generals. His lower-middle-class edginess made him ill at ease in the company of gentlemen – Nevile Henderson, for example, filled him with unease. One suspects that some self-protective instinct prevented him from choosing a medical adviser who might at some stage prescribe the sedative syringe or even the strait-jacket.

At Christmas 1936, after his *annus mirabilis*, Hitler was uncharacteristically cheerful. The woeful recollections of

Klara Hitler's pathetic demise in Linz at Christmas-time 1907 could not altogether diminish the joy he felt at the list of his triumphs: the reoccupation of the Rhineland with not one casualty; the Olympic Games; the party and the armed forces now firmly under his absolute power. Only one conqueror could not be resisted and that was death itself. In 1935, he had become hoarse. A tiny polyp was removed from his larynx and he had been terrified that it would turn out to be a malignant tumour. Now, as he reached the age which had been his mother's when she died, he engaged a new medical adviser – one who would be with him until the end.

Dr Theo Morell was recommended not by another doctor but by the photographer Heinrich Hoffmann, a friend since the early 1920s. Dr Morell was a skin specialist with a wealthy practice in Berlin's Kurfürstendamm. His client list, perhaps appropriately, included actors and film stars worried about moles, lumps, spots or warts. He was fat and unprepossessing in appearance. His large hands were hairy and the nails were often dirty. He once wiped a table with a bandage before tying it around a patient's arm. Like Hitler himself, Morell was a fantasist and liar of advanced degree. When he was taken into American custody after the war, for example, he claimed to be the true discoverer of penicillin. The secret had been stolen by the British Secret Intelligence Service.[2]

Hoffmann was a procurer of more than just a doctor. It was in his photographic studio that Hitler had met Eva Braun, a seventeen-year-old convent-educated girl who would eventually become his wife. Her devotion to him became intense very early, and she found the demands of his popularity and his political life all but impossible to endure. As his career took him away from her on speaking engagements and made its meteoric swoops upwards, she had many outbursts, and made suicide attempts.

When Hitler first consulted Dr Morell, he was himself suffering from a number of nervous complaints. He had eczema on his feet and legs so sore that he was often unable to wear boots. He had an interrupted sleep pattern. He had gastric problems: pains and cramps in the epigastric region. And, an embarrassing complaint for a man who had been described in the *Völkischer Beobachter* as standing like a statue, beyond the measure of earthly man,[3] Hitler suffered acutely from meteorism: perhaps he did not suffer so acutely as those around him, since meteorism is uncontrolled farting, a condition exacerbated by Hitler's strictly vegetarian diet.

Dr Morell prescribed Dr Köster's Anti-Gas pills, a formula which contained nux vomica, a tiny portion of strychnine. Morell also gave intravenous vitamin injections to supplement Hitler's diet. The treatment appeared to increase his tendency, already pronounced, to bursts of preternatural energy. Morell was an extremely bad doctor. He can perhaps not be blamed for the next miserable nine years of European history, but his contribution did not help. It could be argued that Hitler's medical practitioner had a duty, once Hitler's erratic behaviour became more and more pronounced, to insist on a long period of rest, if not actually to administer a cyanide injection. It was inconceivable that Morell would adopt either course, and this was perhaps the reason Hitler – often against the entreaties of his closest associates – retained the services of this bad doctor to the end. Morell, who (accurately for once) claimed to have been Hitler's 'constant companion' from 1936 to 1945, was the ideal doctor, from Hitler's point of view: that is, he treated the host of psychosomatic symptoms, such as stomach cramps and flatulence, which plagued his distinguished patient, while tactfully overlooking what for most people, as the years went by, would seem most obvious, namely Hitler's mental derangement. The mentally ill who do not in the least want to be cured develop cunning habits of self-protection, and the retention of bad medical advisers, and, of course, cowardly life-companions, is essential to their survival.

Hitler's medical condition might have added to the tragedy of German life, and to the tragic farce of his day-to-day existence. It did not, however, alter his course, which was world conquest and the persecution, and eventual elimination, of the Jews.

As an inevitable European war approached, the Nazis allowed themselves to show, more and more, their truly brutal Brownshirt nature, both in the slow advance of mean-spirited anti-Jewish legislation (by 1939 Jews were banned from public libraries; they were not permitted to possess driving-licences or own domestic animals) and in the more open tolerance by the police and the authorities to thuggish Brownshirt violence against Jewish persons and properties.

In 1938, matters reached a climax of violence in the infamous Broken Glass Night (*Kristallnacht*) of 9–10 November. A seventeen-year-old Polish Jew named Herschel Grynszpan, who had grown up in Germany but was now living in Paris, was seething with anger because his parents had been deported from Germany, where they had settled, to Poland. He picked up a revolver, marched into the German embassy in Paris and shot the first diplomat he met, a minor embassy official named Ernst vom Rath. This was the kind of incident for which the Propaganda Minister, Joseph Goebbels, had been waiting. He claimed that demonstrations against the Jews had broken out spontaneously all over Germany. Hitler decreed that there should be no official pogrom but that if acts of violence against Jews were to happen, the authorities should not intervene to stop them.[4] The nudge and the wink had been given: party officials must not be seen openly organizing the violence, but there was now open season on the Jews.

All over Germany, storm-troopers and party activists were getting drunk in memory of the 1923 Munich putsch. They changed into mufti and set out into the streets with their petrol cans. Very soon almost every synagogue in Germany was in flames. Out of a total of some 9,000 Jewish shops in the entire country, some 7,500 were destroyed. In Esslingen, Brownshirts in mufti broke into the Jewish orphanage in the small hours of the morning armed with axes and sledgehammers and destroyed everything they could find – books, religious insignia, clothes – and set light to them in a huge bonfire. In Treuchtlingen in Franconia, Jews woke to find looters breaking into their houses, smashing furniture. The intruders penetrated the cellars, where they found cowering, terrified families, and smashed wine bottles and jars of preserves. Everywhere, all over the country, there was terror and mayhem. It is impossible to estimate the numbers killed – perhaps as many as 2,000. At least 300 Jews committed suicide. Following direct orders from Hitler, Jews were set upon and humiliated. In Saarbrücken, men's beards were set alight, while others were forced to dance in front of the smouldering remains of their synagogue. Others were drenched with hosepipes. Between 9 and 16 November, 30,000 Jewish men were arrested and transported to concentration camps at Dachau, Buchenwald and Sachsenhausen where they had to sleep on the floor in straw wearing, in that November cold, only shirts and trousers.[5] Beatings were regular and by the end of the year 276 men had died in custody.

Hitler's anti-Jewish mania, in all its murderous intensity, now became an open part, not merely of party rallies, but of his rhetoric in international diplomacy. On 21 January 1939, he told the Czechoslovakian Foreign Minister, 'The Jews among us will be annihilated.' And on 30 January, he told the Reichstag:

> I have been a prophet all my life and I was mostly laughed at. In the time of my struggle for power it was in the first place the Jewish people who received with nothing but laughter my prophecy that one day I would take over the leadership of the

state and with it the whole people and then among many other things bring the Jewish problem to its solution. I believe that the roars of laughter of those days may well have suffocated in the throats of the Jews in the meantime.

I want to be a prophet again today: if international finance Jewry in Europe and beyond should succeed once more in plunging the peoples into a world war, then the result will not be the Bolshevization of the earth and thus the victory of Jewry, but the annihilation of the Jewish race in Europe.[6]

What Hitler was saying was quite clear. The words were broadcast over and over again. No one in the world could mistake them. The Jews were now being held hostage. If anyone dared put up an armed struggle against his desire for world domination, the Jews would pay the price.

Franklin D. Roosevelt delivered a pious speech denouncing Broken Glass Night but the Americans continued to insist on immigration controls and to view the influx of refugees from Germany with dismay. The shaming truth is that the international community did very little, even by way of verbal protest, still less in practical ways, to help the German Jews before the war. Sir Horace Wilson, industrial adviser to Neville Chamberlain, was one of the chief negotiators with Hitler during the tortuous series of diplomatic crises which led up to the war. At the very last hour, in the summer of 1939, Sir Horace, at Chamberlain's behest, held secret talks with Fritz Hesse, a representative of German Foreign Minister Ribbentrop. The British offered Germany a twenty-five-year defensive alliance, and the eventual return of the German colonies, if aggressive action in Europe could cease. This was in August 1939.[7] Absolutely no mention was made of the plight of the Jews. Indeed, when being interviewed in 1968 by the journalist Colin Cross, Sir Horace confessed that he could understand Hitler's feelings about the Jews. 'Have you ever met a Jew you liked?' asked Sir Horace.

Western politicians, post-dating their cheques, like to suppose that the world expressed horror at Nazi anti-Semitism before the war. In the run-up to the invasion of Iraq by US and British forces in 2003, the British Prime Minister Tony Blair actually stated that the British had gone to war in 1939 to protect the Jews. The truth is that the voices of public figures, such as Winston Churchill or the radical MP Josiah Wedgwood who spoke out in the 1930s against German anti-Semitism, were in a tiny minority.

What held Europe, and the world, in a state of scarcely tolerable suspense during the years 1938 and 1939 was not the fate of the German Jews, nor even the belief that Hitler meant what he said when he promised to annihilate world Jewry. It was the possibility that, as a result of diplomatic failure, Europe, and then the world, would once again be drawn into what an older generation had vowed would never happen again: war.

There were four major diplomatic crises, and in the first three, Hitler played a stylish and victorious poker game. A memorandum of August 1936, sent by Hitler to Göring, with a copy to Blomberg, the War Minister, spoke of war being inevitable by 1940. He wrote in these terms because he had been informed that Germany was running out of foreign currency to pay for imports, and in particular for oil cake, needed by the Ministry of Agriculture, and oil and rubber, needed for military purposes. On 4 September the Cabinet was told, 'the Plan is based on the assumption that war with Russia is inevitable'.[8]

There was never any doubt in Hitler's mind that the conquest of Eastern Europe, and the invasion of Russia, was the Napoleonic end which would set a seal upon his greatness. On 23 August, Germany signed a pact with the Soviet Union to carve up Poland between them, Hitler having the German-speaking area adjacent to Danzig (present-day Gdansk), and Stalin having the Slavic-speaking regions to the east. Hitler had no intention, however, of preserving a long-term alliance with Stalin, much as he admired the brutality of Stalin as a leader. His assurances to Stalin of friendship and brotherhood were as trustworthy as his promises in 1923 that he would never contemplate a putsch, or his assurances to the German people in 1933 that he did not wish to establish a dictatorship, or his assurances to the gullible British politicians and diplomats during 1937–9 that if he were only allowed to invade this or that part of Europe, he would settle down peacefully with his neighbours. Lying was part of Hitler's nature. It is this fact, obvious with hindsight to absolutely everyone, which gives such pathos to the view expressed by Neville Chamberlain, when he had visited the Berghof to debate the future of Czechoslovakia with the

German Leader: 'In spite of the heartlessness and ruthless-ness I thought I saw in his face, I got the impression that here was a man who could be relied upon when he had given his word.'⁹

Josiah Wedgwood was one of the very few politicians to tell Chamberlain the truth. 'Those who are anxious for the survival of this world, of justice, of freedom and democracy trust the German Chancellor less than ever, and quite frankly we regard those who do trust him as fools and traitors to the cause of democracy.'¹⁰

The four great crises concerned – (1) the annexation of Austria; (2) the annexation of the German-speaking Sudetenland – hitherto part of the new European state of Czechoslovakia; (3) the dismantlement of Czechoslovakia itself; and (4) the annexation of Danzig and western Poland, which were the former territories of Frederick the Great in East Prussia.

The Anschluss with Austria, given the nature of the times, and Hitler's own background, was inevitable. Hitler summoned the Austrian Chancellor, Schuschnigg, to the Berghof in February 1938, and more or less issued him with an ultimatum. When Schuschnigg protested, Hitler threw a tantrum. When Schuschnigg protested that if the Germans were to invade Austria, it would mean a European war, Hitler very plausibly scoffed. No one, he correctly averred – not Britain, not France, not America, not Italy – would lift a finger to save Austria. It was appalling for Austrian patriots, Austrian Jews, the more thoughtful Austrian Catholics; but when the invasion actually happened, the German troops were greeted with an ecstatic welcome. In Vienna, outside the Austrian Chancellery, an estimated 100,000 people gathered on the night of the German invasion to cheer, and to shout – 'Down with the Jews! Heil Hitler! Hang Schuschnigg!' It would have been strange, in such circumstances, for the international community to rally round and 'liberate' an Austria which had responded in this way to invasion.

When Hitler visited his home town of Linz, another crowd of 100,000 were waiting for him outside the City Hall. Here was the town where, as a whey-faced shy boy, he had wandered about in love with Stefanie. Here he had attended the operas of Wagner with his friend Kubizek and talked of his plans to be an architect or a great artist. Here his beloved mother, Klara, had died. Tears cascaded down his cheeks as he saw the enthusiasm of the crowds. And no one who witnessed it, and contemplated in how brief a time the poor man of Linz had become a world-dominator, could fail to feel the prodigious nature of what had happened.

As so often was the case with Hitler, his own inner fantasy life had been imposed upon the world. To this extent, the Anschluss was more like a piece of theatrical direction than it was an act of war. He had begun *My Struggle* with a reflection upon the providential nature of the fact that he had been born as a borderer. The very first paragraph stated the need for unification. 'German-Austria must once more be reunited with the great German Motherland: and not just for economic reasons. No, no! ... One Blood belongs together in

One Reich.' A mere fifteen years before, he had dictated these words to the faithful, bushy-browed Hess, who had typed them out for all to read. And now the swastika hung over the Realschule in Linz where Hitler and Wittgenstein had been to school; over the Vienna Riding Stables and the State Opera. Austria, the nurse of so much great European art and literature, was in the grip of a party that burned books. Vienna, the city of Alban Berg, Gustav Klimt, Gustav Mahler and Sigmund Freud, had submitted to the party which burned books.

Such was the nature of the times. Mussolini alone among European leaders could have stopped Hitler's advance, and he deliberately failed to do so, knowing that the German Leader's friendship would be useful to him.

The next gamble in 1938 was a much riskier one. The Sudeten Germans were demanding an Anschluss such as had taken place with Austria. The fact that they were part of the newly created nation of Czechoslovakia was the consequence of the Treaty of Versailles, and their desire for union with the Reich was perfectly understandable. On the other hand, Czechoslovakia had been, among all the countries of Mittel-Europa, a successful experiment in building a modern industrial democracy. There were many, inside and outside Czechoslovakia, who cherished this, and who would not want the nation, new and artificially created as it might have been, to be absorbed into the Nazi police state.

Hitler had to decide two things. First was whether France and Britain would allow him to annex the German

Sudetenland without threatening war. Second, if he got away with doing this, whether he could then proceed to dismantle Czechoslovakia altogether.

The British Prime Minister, Neville Chamberlain, and his Foreign Secretary, Lord Halifax, were singularly ill-equipped to negotiate with Hitler. History so hates what they did, and what they did not do, that it damns their policy of appeasing Hitler as cowardly. In fact, their appeasement had something of double-think about it. While doing everything in their power to avoid the outbreak of hostilities, they were in fact arming for war. Far more aircraft, for example, were produced in Britain in 1938 and 1939 than were rolling off the German production-lines.

Edvard Beneš, the Czechoslovakian President, was a much stronger character than the Austrian Schuschnigg. He also had the misplaced hope that the French and the British would, if necessary, consider military intervention if Hitler threatened Czechoslovakia. It remains one of the great imponderables of history. What would have happened if Chamberlain and Daladier, the French premier, had moved in troops and tanks and planes to help the Czechs? Had they done so, Hitler would almost certainly have at least held back; and the valuable coal-fields, mineral resources and highly skilled armed forces of Czechoslovakia would have remained at the disposal of the Allies if or when later hostility came. Perhaps that hostility would never have come and, having called Hitler's bluff, the Allies would have been able to look back on 1938 as the apogee of his military ambitions …

But this was not how events played out. On 15 September, Chamberlain flew to Munich to discuss the problem with Hitler. They agreed that the Sudeten Germans should be given a plebiscite to decide their own future. On 19 September, the French and the British presented Beneš with a cowardly plan to secede the Sudetenland to Hitler. Before Hitler had advanced a single tank, or even advanced a paper proposition for the annexation of the Sudetenland, Chamberlain and Halifax did it for him. Hitler had played for time, hoping that they might be forced, if by no other force than shame, to honour their treaty obligation to protect Czechoslovakia. In London, Chamberlain spoke by radio broadcast on 27 September 1938: 'How horrible, fantastic, incredible it is that we should be digging trenches and trying on gas masks here because of a quarrel in a far away country between people of whom we know nothing.' Two days later, he flew to Munich for a conference with Hitler, Mussolini, Daladier and Ribbentrop. The Czechs were excluded from the discussions. Hitler could not believe that Chamberlain and Daladier – 'little worms' he called them – had agreed so easily to his terms.

Six months later, in March 1939, Hitler invaded the rest of Czechoslovakia, incorporating Bohemia and Moravia into a 'protectorate' and installing a puppet government in Slovakia. His pretext was that he needed to quell 'unrest' on Germany's frontiers.

He had now won three great victories without a shot being fired – he had annexed Austria, annexed the Sudetenland, and destroyed Czechoslovakia. There remained one more round of the poker game: he wanted the German-speaking city of Danzig.

There was really no reason for him to suppose that the British and the French, who had behaved with such cowardice over Czechoslovakia, would risk a war over Poland. And herein is the reason for anger with Chamberlain and Daladier. Had they had heeded Beneš's call and been prepared to fight for Czechoslovakia, Hitler would have been far less likely to go on taking risks, and therefore he would have been in no position to become the master of Western Europe by the summer of 1940. But that is only one way of viewing things. And the other was provocatively encapsulated by A. J. P. Taylor in his much-hated and controversial book, *The Origins of the Second World War*: 'In 1938, Czechoslovakia was betrayed. In 1939 Poland was saved. Less than one hundred thousand Czechs died during the war. Six and a half million Poles were killed. Which was better – to be a betrayed Czech or a saved Pole?'

Taylor's brilliant-sounding paradox overlooks (a) the number of Polish Jews included in this statistic; and (b) the appalling folly of Chamberlain allowing Hitler to possess the Czech army, their military hardware, their coal mines and their steelworks, all of which could well have been enough, had it remained in the hands of Beneš and the free Czechs, to stay Hitler's hand when it came to war.

But tempting as it is to play parlour games, history in the end only concerns what did happen and not what might have happened. What did happen is that Hitler, encouraged by his success with the little worms at Munich, invaded Poland in September 1939. So many public declarations had been made by Britain and France that they would not tolerate this piece of aggression that even Chamberlain could not stand by and let it happen.

Moreover, Hitler joined Mussolini in the Pact of Steel, a treaty of friendship and co-operation, signed on 22 May. But the Leader's most extraordinary diplomatic coup came three months later, on 23 August, when Molotov, the new Soviet Foreign Minister, signed a non-aggression pact with Germany. This was the preliminary to Hitler and Stalin carving up Poland. Hitler's non-aggression pact with the Russians was totally mendacious, and it in no way suggested that he had changed his mind about invading the Soviet Union.

The invasion of Poland took place on 3 September. It was the turning point of Hitler's life. Hitherto, since the First World War, his career had been one of meteoric ascendance. No wonder, in all his bombastic rhetoric, he felt that Destiny or Providence was guiding him. He had achieved a 'bloodless revolution' at home, and within the last three years of the decade, he had managed to annex, without a shot being fired, extensive territories which it would have taken the most successful military conqueror in modern German history, Frederick the Great, years of war to accomplish. It really seemed as if Providence was on Hitler's side.

But so, too, was a huge majority of the German people. The Swiss psychiatrist Carl Gustav Jung, who spent years discussing Hitler's character with Ernst Hanfstaengl, thought that Hitler 'is the first man to tell every German what he has been thinking and feeling all along in his unconscious about German fate, especially since the defeat in the World War, and the one characteristic which colours every German soul is the typically German inferiority complex, the complex of the younger brother, of the one who is always a bit late to the feast. Hitler's power is not political; it is *magic*.'[11]

When he instigated the invasion of Poland, this magic began to desert Hitler. In so far as Jung was right that Hitler enjoyed an extraordinary rapport with 'every German', it was in his belief that the miseries and disgrace of the previous two decades could be wiped out peacefully. The public were then prepared to turn a blind eye when Jews had their shop windows smashed. Or they actually enjoyed the cruelty. Hitler was a man who had restored the economy, brought full employment, and restored to Germany its pre-war territories in the Rhineland and the Sudetenland.

When the panzer divisions moved over the eastern borders towards Danzig, the crowds in Berlin were shocked. The outbreak of the First World War had been greeted in all the capitals of Europe with cheering and patriotic enthusiasm. Hitler himself was captured on camera among the cheering crowds in Munich in 1914. The outbreak of war in 1939 was received in Berlin with stunned dread and silence. There were no cheering crowds. The magic departed at that hour.

Hitler had offered his people tremendous simplicities – revenge for the Treaty of Versailles, '*Lebensraum*', Jew-baiting, employment, a fast road and a little car for every God-fearing *kleinbürgerlich* family in the Reich. It was a winning formula for as long as the sons and fathers of the Reich did not have to risk their lives in battle.

There had always been another Hitler, of course, as well as the man that Gertrude Stein in 1937 had deemed worthy of the Nobel Peace Prize.[12] That was the Wagnerian mystic who inhabited the strange mythologies of Germanic legend, the stories which ended with the dragon unleashed, the great World-Tree Yggdrasil pulled to the ground, and the fortress of the Gods themselves, Valhalla, reduced to a flaming ruin.

On the eve of war, Hitler visited his old friend Winifred Wagner and attended a performance of *The Valkyrie* at the Festspielhaus in Bayreuth. Winifred had been one of Hitler's loyal supporters from the beginning, and she would never waver in her devotion. But this was, as it happened, one of the last evenings the old friends spent together. The British Ambassador, Sir Nevile Henderson, was also, on 30 July 1939, attending *The Valyrkie* and Winifred Wagner, British by birth, German in spirit, implored Hitler to share a box with him. Hitler replied that he could not allow himself to be compromised. The Ring Cycle was completed on 2 August, when Hitler saw *Götterdämmerung*. The singer Marta Fuchs, in the reception afterwards, asked him in her Swabian accent – 'You ain't goin' to make war, are you, my Leader?' 'You can believe me, Frau Fuchs, there will be no war', said Hitler.[13]

By then he knew this was a lie, and another orchestra was playing in his soul, a drama in which easy victories were reserved for the mean and lowly; and in which the true glory, of fire and of blood, was found in the huge orgasmic music of self-destruction.

EIGHT

1939–1941 War Lord

An older generation in England sometimes spoke of 'Hitler's War', to distinguish it from the First World War. In many senses, the Second World War was indeed Hitler's war. Against military advice at home, and diplomatic pleadings from abroad, he had launched the invasion of Poland. And now, not only Germany, but the other countries of Europe, and eventually of the world, were to be caught up in Hitler's scheme. Whatever the appeasers in England might have hoped before 3 September 1939, once war broke out, only three options remained: either Hitler would be defeated; or he would be totally successful; or – a fantasy-option, as hindsight makes clear, but one to which, for example, Lord Halifax clung until 1941 – there would be a period of fighting, and then a ceasefire, after which Hitler would continue to control Europe while Britain retained her empire in the rest of the world.

Lord Halifax's fantasy was almost certainly one which Hitler himself shared. He had been taken by surprise when the 'little worms', Chamberlain and Daladier, declared war on him merely because he had sent the panzer divisons to reclaim Danzig for Prussia. The first part of 'Hitler's War' – from 1939 to 1941 – was, in a sense, an anti-climactic prelude to his real war aim: the invasion and conquest of Russia.

During the first nine months of the war it seemed as if the same outstanding good luck which had blessed his life as a peacetime leader would continue to buoy Hitler's career as a warlord. In a sense, however, the success was disconcerting. It was not what he had planned, and it must have been fairly clear to any of the military top brass that Germany's economy, and Germany's fighting power, could not sustain a war on two fronts. His decision in 1941 to invade Russia before he had thoroughly defeated Britain was a major tactical blunder.

But despite horrible losses of life on both sides in those early months it looked as though Hitler's victory would be swift. A key moment was his successful invasion of neutral Norway in April 1940. Both sides in the war saw the strategic importance of Norway in a naval war. From October 1939, Grand Admiral Erich Raeder urged the conquest upon Hitler as a way of protecting the transportation of iron ore from the Gällivare mines in northern Sweden to Germany and establishing U-boat bases along the fjords, especially at Trondheim. Also, Sweden was never going to come into the war against Germany, whereas King Haakon VII of Norway was pro-British – and in the event escaped Norway in time to form a government in exile in London. At the Nuremberg trials, Admiral Raeder was prosecuted for violating Norway's neutrality, a charge which many saw as the hypocrisy of 'victor's justice'.[1] The British were as anxious as the Germans to disturb this neutrality. The Germans simply outwitted them. British troops were sent to the fjords with heavy field guns and no equipment to get them to the tops of the cliffs. Some British soldiers, in the freezing spring weather, were issued with tropical kit to confuse the enemy. Others were wearing Arctic boots from 1919 that were several sizes too large.

Talking to his military colleagues the next year, Hitler saw the Norwegian campaign as decisive. 'I cannot understand even in retrospect, how it was that the powerful British Navy did not succeed in defeating, or at least in hindering, an operation which did not have even the support of the very modest German forces. If the Norwegian campaign had failed, we should not have been able to create the conditions which were a pre-requisite for the success of our submarines.'[2]

All this was true. The truth only redoubles the paradox of the events of that summer. The calamity of the Norwegian campaign can be laid squarely at the door of the First Lord of the Admiralty in London, Winston Churchill. Yet its total failure led to a vote in the House of Commons of no confidence, not in Churchill, but in the Prime Minister, Neville Chamberlain. This in turn led to Chamberlain's resignation and his replacement by Churchill, who would prove to be Hitler's nemesis.

Norway fell in April 1940. In the next two months, Denmark was defeated. The Netherlands, Belgium and

Luxembourg fell. And, on 20 June, France conceded defeat. Both militarily and psychologically, it was a moment that Hitler needed to reach if he was to undo the humiliations of the Treaty of Versailles. No one, however, on either side, could have predicted that he would achieve his object so soon.

He did not do so without loss of life. These summer campaigns saw grievous casualties on both sides. About 1.5 million French troops were passed into German captivity in that humiliating June. And the reason why the French capitulated, and why the hero of Verdun, General Pétain, told them to lay down their arms, was quite simple. They could not tolerate a repetition of the slaughter which France had seen, on its own soil, during the long trench warfare of 1914–18. The Germans had lost 27,000 men in the short campaign, with 111,000 wounded. The French had lost a crippling 92,000 with over 200,000 wounded. The British Expeditionary Force (BEF) had lost 11,000 men killed and with 14,000 wounded. They limped to retreat at Dunkirk where they were rescued by Royal Navy vessels and by a flotilla of 'little boats' – pleasure steamers and the like. The catastrophe was celebrated as if it were some kind of triumph, and the 'Dunkirk spirit' is still invoked today as a synonym for British *esprit de corps*. But the Dunkirk spirit had left Hitler the master of Europe.

On 22 June, at Compiègne, fifty miles north-east of Paris, in the same railway carriage where the Germans had themselves surrendered to the French in 1918, French General Charles Huntziger signed the French surrender. The American radio correspondent William Shirer, watching through binoculars, caught Hitler's expression at that scene. 'I have seen that face many times at the great moments of his life. But today! It is afire with scorn, anger, hate, revenge, triumph.'[3]

When he visited Paris, Hitler was of course cock-a-hoop, but in a provincial, autodidactic manner which must secretly have embarrassed the more sophisticated Albert Speer, the architect summoned to be at his side. 'I love Paris', said Hitler guilelessly, 'it has been a place of artistic importance since the nineteenth century' – the sort of remark you can imagine passing between the sixteen-year-old Hitler and his friend Kubizek in Linz, but which, made by a fifty-year-old man, was embarrassing. 'Like you, I would have studied here', he blustered, 'if Fate had not pushed me into politics, since my ambitions before the First World War were in the field of art.' Free now, as a world-conqueror, to rewrite history, he omitted to mention that another consideration was that he had failed to get into art school and had been congenitally lazy.

A high point of his visit to Paris was at Napoleon's tomb in Les Invalides, where, with a cap held respectfully to his breast, he paid tribute to the last megalomaniac to attempt the domination of all Europe. To Hermann Giesler, the other architect brought along with Speer to accompany the Leader to Paris, he said, 'You will design my tomb.' Flushed with Napoleonic fervour, and to celebrate the victory over the French, Hitler created, Napoleon-style, twelve new Field Marshals, but one of them, Wilhelm Keitel, could have spoken for them all when he said, 'I had no authority. I was Field

Marshal in name only. I had no troops, no authority – only to carry out Hitler's orders.' He was speaking to a psychiatrist at Nuremberg in 1945, after his master was dead and his country was in ruins.

With Europe at his feet, Hitler had to decide what to do about the puzzling British. Less than a year earlier, they had been offering him terms of peace on the sole condition that he would keep out of Poland. They had then joined forces with the French, and historical opinion remains divided as to whether or not Hitler committed a blunder in allowing the BEF to escape at Dunkirk, or whether he was deliberately letting them off lightly in the hope of negotiating a peaceful armistice with the government in Westminster.

Winston Churchill, the new Prime Minister, was a passionate Francophile and one of his first acts on taking office had been an attempt to send all available British fighter planes to assist the French in their last struggle. Had he done so, it is difficult to see what would have prevented Hitler from invading Britain in the late summer of 1940, inflicting heavy losses in battles on the British mainland, and, presumably, winning the war. As Churchill announced his scheme in the Cabinet room, the Chief of the Air Staff, Sir Cyril Newall, and the Leader of the Liberal Party, Archibald Sinclair, were attempting to point out to Churchill the disaster which would ensue if his plan were followed. The insults which were being heaped on their heads by the new Prime Minister were, in the view of one present, 'unbelievable'. Like Hitler, Churchill was able to get his own way by bullying those around him into submission. Unlike Hitler, he did occasionally have the grace to listen to reason. Just as he was on the point of telephoning the French premier and promising British planes, Sir Hugh Dowding, Commander in Chief of Fighter Command in the Royal Air Force, got to his feet '… and taking my graph with me, I walked round to the seat occupied by the Prime Minister. I laid the graph on the table in front of him, and I said, "If the present rate of wastage continues another fortnight, we shall not have a single Hurricane left in France or in this country." I laid particular emphasis on "or in this country".' [4]

Churchill saw reason. The Battle of Britain was won in the air by the 'few' – the fighter pilots with Spitfires and Hurricanes. The British got the better of the fighting, largely because they had pioneered the use of radar. After two weeks of heroic fighting on both sides, as August came to an end, a German bomber, a Heinkel HE-11, instead of bombing the British airfields, dropped its load on London docks, probably by mistake. Churchill's bruiser mentality made an immediate, highly controversial, decision. He would commit the war crime of bombing civilians.

On 26 August 1940, eighty-one RAF bombers flew over Berlin and unleashed their deadly load. There would still have been a chance, at this stage – albeit a small one – of Göring's Luftwaffe concentrating all its energy on the defeat of the Hurricanes and Spitfires in the air over Britain and thereby winning control. But Churchill's brutal mind had accurately read Hitler's bullying nature. 'When they declare that they will attack our cities in great strength, then we will eradicate their cities', Hitler promised, in a typical piece of hyperbole.

By diverting the bombers from the airfields – where they would have destroyed British fighter planes – to British cities, where (as in German cities) civilian anger at the aerial bombardment hardened patriotic resolve, Hitler made a fundamental error of tactical judgement. By late September, the 'Blitz' had begun in London, with Buckingham Palace and Westminster Abbey and many of the Wren City churches satisfyingly – from Hitler's viewpoint – ablaze. But the Battle of Britain had been lost. When Göring asked a young flying ace, Colonel Adolf Galland, what he needed to win, he replied, 'an outfit of Spitfires for my group'. Göring marched off, growling as he went.[5]

By allowing the bombardment of civilians, and at a comparatively early stage of the war, Churchill behaved with a brutality which Hitler was only too prepared to match. More than any other war in history, this was one which involved everyone: not merely soldiers and airmen in battle, but citizens of all ages, huddling in air-raid shelters by night, and by day prepared – in munitions factories, in voluntary work as air-raid wardens, and in innumerable other ways – to 'do their bit'. For as long as the Leader's escapades led to prodigious victory abroad, Hitler retained his popularity with the Germans. But the old adulation was to be from now onwards sporadic and conditional, as it was with Churchill.

The faithful Hess – *mein* Hesserl, as Hitler called him, the second Kubizek, the Leader's chum, and in consequence, the

Deputy Leader, who had been with Hitler in Landsberg Prison, and typed out *My Struggle* – what a task! – had begun to have visions of lines of coffins and grieving mothers: the realities of war. More than a little crazy, Hess had consulted soothsayers and astrologers and the auguries were not good. True, the war appeared to be going well for the Germans during 1941. Hungary, with its large pro-Nazi population, had joined with the Reich. The difficult invasion of Greece was accomplished. Yugoslavia was crushed – the codename for that part of the campaign was PUNISHMENT.

Hess might have been crazy, but he and his astrologers were not deceived. The future was spattered with blood, littered with corpses; not thousands, but millions. Old flying ace from the First World War that he was, Hess did not believe that the war with Britain was necessary, and he was convinced that if he intervened, and sued for peace, it would be a way of saving lives. Through a member of the anti-Nazi resistance movement, called Albrecht Haushofer, Hess was persuaded that if he were to fly to Scotland and have secret talks with the Duke of Hamilton – a senior Scottish peer, known to both Churchill and the King – there would surely be the chance of, if not peace, then at least the talk of peace. After all, less than two years had passed since Sir Horace Wilson had confided in the Germans the offer, fashioned by Chamberlain and Halifax, that the British would do more or less anything to make peace.

By 1941, however, this was the last thing which either Hitler or Churchill wanted. Perhaps Hess partly knew this. He was a brave, foolhardy man. He set out on the venture without having once practised a parachute jump, and he realized when he was in mid-air at the controls of his Messerschmitt Me-110 that he did not know how to position the plane before making such a jump. Not surprisingly, he broke his ankle upon his descent. After the farce of arriving in Scotland and being arrested by the Home Guard, Hess was eventually interviewed by the Lord Chancellor Sir John Simon and Lord Beaverbrook – now Air Minister as well as being in charge of the Churchill propaganda machine. Hess must have realized as soon as he met these two that his mission was in vain, that there would be no chance of Churchill negotiating a peace with Germany and that the only way for the war to end was by the scale of mass slaughter which he had most hoped to avoid. He was taken to the Tower of London and spent the rest of his days in captivity, after the war being kept in Spandau Prison by the Russians until his nineties, of no harm to anyone.

Hitler's anger, when he heard of *mein* Hesserl's escapade, had a slow boil. At first he spoke with wistful melancholy of his lost friend. Then the rage began to build. 'Hess is first of all, a deserter, and if I ever catch him, he will pay for this as any ordinary traitor. Furthermore, it seems to me that this step was strongly influenced by the astrological cliques which Hess kept around him.' Hitler gave orders at once that astrology should be banned.[6] It had somehow come to his attention that Lord Rothermere's newspapers, the *Daily Mail* in particular, had horoscopes. Many readers of the *Daily Mail* must have wondered how seriously they were meant to take these astrological speculations. He spoke about a year later of 'the horoscope in which the Anglo-Saxons in particular have great faith'. Rather than thinking of horoscopes as a harmless game, he saw them as 'a swindle whose significance must not be underestimated'.[7]

The propaganda machine went into overdrive to blacken the name of Rudolf Hess. He was in the grip of astrologers. He kept a pet lion. He was half-cracked. All of it was true, but, precisely because it was true, it begged the question of why Hitler had considered him a suitable person to be the Deputy Leader of the German dictatorship. Hess might have seemed deranged, but there was, at least, in his air-borne peace-mission, an ill-judged desire to save human life – not a consideration which seems to have worried Joseph Goebbels, as he limped about on his club foot and called for more and more Jews to be slaughtered; or Hermann Göring in his ever-more elaborate Ruritanian uniforms; or the sinister, bespectacled Heinrich Himmler. Well could you believe the despondent diarist Reck-Malleczewen, who wrote, of the progress of the war, 'behind all this horror ... there lies concealed a cosmic process, a gigantic psychosis and the unleashing of a horde of demons'.[8]

One of the fears of the demon-band was that Hess would have blurted out their secret plan to invade Russia. But Hess had as usual been prepared to lie for his master and hero. When asked directly by Sir John Simon, he had assured the Lord Chancellor that 'there is no foundation for the rumours now being spread that Hitler is contemplating an early attack on Russia'.[9] He said that on 10 June 1941.

Even as he spoke, huge numbers of troops were moving towards Germany's eastern frontiers. By 22 June, Hitler's Napoleonic message had been sent to them: 'German soldiers! You are about to join battle, a hard and crucial battle. The destiny of Europe and the future of the German Reich, the existence of our nation, now lies in your hands alone.'[10]

He never spoke a truer word. Barbarossa, as the invasion of the Soviet Union was codenamed, unleashed the greatest, bloodiest and most difficult land campaign ever fought in the history of warfare. The failure of the German army to conquer Russia did indeed guarantee that Germany as a nation would be destroyed and that the eastern half of Europe would remain in bondage to the Communists until 1989. The tragic paradox at the centre of mid- to late-twentieth-century history is that Europe, and the world, owed its deliverance from the tyranny of Hitler to the heroism of the Red Army. Of course, Britain's resistance to Hitler in 1940 played its part at the beginning of the conflict, as did the enormous contribution of men and arms by the United States when they eventually entered the conflict. But the Russian contribution was crucial: it was the resistance of the Russian people to invasion, siege and starvation, and the preparedness of Stalin to sacrifice millions of lives, both military and civilian in what Russians still call the Great Patriotic War, which secured Hitler's defeat. To be delivered from the tyranny of Hitler, it was necessary to be delivered into the tyranny of Josef Stalin.

If you were a Pole, a Czech, an East German, a Hungarian, a Serb or a Croat you did not have to be A. J. P. Taylor to see that this was a questionable form of liberation.

Hitler was the mastermind behind the Russian campaign. It was a blunder of enormous proportions to have undertaken it while Britain was still left undefeated. But he thrilled to the task. The very fact that his own generals were so uncertain about the outcome of Barbarossa filled him with confidence. And – at last – he was up against an enemy whom he could truly respect. Unlike Chamberlain and Daladier, the 'little worms', or Churchill, 'a superannuated drunkard sustained by Jewish gold', here was another mass-murderer, Stalin, who 'must command our unconditional respect. In his own way he is the hell of a fellow! He knows his models, Genghis Khan and the others, very well.'[11] When Hitler's henchmen heard him expound this view at his headquarters, the Wolf's Lair, in July 1942, they must, whatever their degree of loyalty to the Leader, have felt a chill pass through them. They must have realized that their Leader, to whom they had looked as a deliverer of easy victories, was now looking towards a future in which mass slaughter, far from being seen as undesirable, was a 'model' to be followed. To such a man, gore-stained glory, more than victory, was to become an aim.

The immense strength and skill of the Red Army and the titanic heroism of the Russian people in resisting invasion must have taken Hitler by surprise. To the reader sixty and more years later, the sheer scale of the campaign is not possible to absorb. Within one day, German attacks had demolished a quarter of the entire Soviet air force. Within four months, the Germans had occupied 600,000 square miles of Russian soil, captured 3 million Russian troops, butchered countless Jews and other civilians as they went, and come within sixty-five miles of Moscow. But within a further four months, more than 200,000 German soldiers had been killed, a staggering 726,000 wounded, and a further 113,000 incapacitated by frostbite.

In August 1941, Hitler made the decision that the German army should capture Kiev, rather than pressing on against fearsome odds to capture Moscow itself. It was another grievous tactical mistake. Kiev fell, with 665,000 Soviet prisoners taken by the Germans. Leningrad was besieged in September 1941, leading to some of the most terrible scenes of human carnage ever witnessed on European soil: 226 citizens arrested for cannibalism, while the bombs rained down for month after month, while thousands died of starvation in the cold, and putrefied bodies lay frozen in the ice.

Hitler's *Table Talk* is perhaps revealing in this respect. While he condemned millions of his fellow human beings to the sufferings of that campaign, which had come about solely because of his belief that Russia would provide the German peoples with *Lebensraum*, he discoursed in August 1942 – that is, after that winter of countless deaths and horrifying misery – on his own capacity to endure the cold:

Having to change into long trousers was always a misery to me. Even with a temperature of below zero I used to go about in lederhosen. The feeling of freedom they give you is wonderful. Abandoning my shorts was one of the biggest sacrifices I had to make ... Anything up to five degrees below zero I didn't even notice. Quite a number of young people today already wear shorts all the year round; it is just a question of habit. In the future I shall have an SS Highland Brigade in lederhosen!

By the end of 1941, Hitler's War had indeed become a World War. Very few countries remained outside the conflict. One which did was Spain. Although Hitler had sent planes and ammunition to help General Franco overcome the legal republican government of Spain in 1937, the cunning Spaniard would not repay his debt and enter the world war on Germany's side. Mussolini, however, had taken Italy to war against Britain and France on 10 June 1940. This remains one of the most puzzling aspects of the war since no reason had ever existed why these countries should feel the remotest hostility towards one another.

Japan was an ally of Hitler, but he never really saw how it could be useful to him. When the Japanese Foreign Minister, Yōsuke Matsuoka, a graduate of the University of Oregon, visited Hitler in the summer of 1941, the German Leader urged upon him the desirability of attacking Singapore. This was because of Hitler's obsession with the British Empire. The fact that a small nation of 45 million could control an empire of over 600 million people throughout the world filled him with envy, and after two years of war with Britain he saw Japan primarily as a way of undermining Britain. He did not see that Japan would be a useful ally against Russia, and that, had Japan attacked Siberia at the moment he launched his Barbarossa campaign, there would have been a real chance of defeating the Soviet Union. With his typical deviousness, Hitler did not even mention his Russian invasion plans when Matsuoka visited him days before the Barbarossa offensive. Matsuoka resigned as Foreign Minister not long after in protest over Japan's refusal to engage on the Siberian front.

The Japanese were in the war for what they could get out of it. They did not want a long, drawn-out conflict, still less a mutually assured plan of world-destruction. As early as 1942, Emperor Hirohito was instructing his Prime Minister, Tojo, 'not to miss any opportunity to terminate the war'.[12]

But it was the Japanese who had made the war a truly global conflict some months earlier. On 7 December 1941 they bombed Pearl Harbor in Hawaii, destroying a sizeable proportion of the American fleet. Had more ships been in harbour that morning, the Japanese might have had some chance, eventually, of winning a war against the United States in the Far East. As it was, they brought into the war a rich, huge enemy, who had now finally been forced to side with Britain and its empire against Hitler. The Japanese thereby released Stalin from any fear that he would be attacked on his eastern front.

Hitler, unable to appreciate the blow which the Japanese had unwittingly struck against their own side, was exultant. 'We cannot lose this war! Now we have a partner who has not been defeated in three thousand years!' On the basis of this flimsy piece of history, Hitler proceeded to compound the blunder of invading Russia. Having allowed his anti-Jewish mania to blind him to the extreme anti-Semitism of the American establishment, the strength of isolationism in the United States Senate and the unwillingness of the American public to engage in a world war, he decided that Roosevelt was being manipulated by a gang of Jews. For this ridiculous and inaccurate reason, he declared war on the United States of America, and thereby sealed his own doom.

NINE

The Final Solution

Hitler did not invent anti-Semitism. He told the readers of *My Struggle* that when he first went to Vienna as a young man, he was shocked by the anti-Semitic tone of the Austrian newspapers, 'which seemed to me unworthy of the cultural tradition of a great nation'.[1] By the end of the book, however, he had come to accept, with a manic fervour, all the clichés of anti-Semitic belief: that a Jewish conspiracy lay behind both the capitalism swindle, and the Bolshevik attempt to overthrow that swindle; that the Jews were conspiring to undermine the European nations by impregnating their women, pocketing their savings, and corrupting their morality by spreading syphilis, modern art and trade unionism.

'With satanic joy in his face, the black-haired Jewish youth lurks in wait for the unsuspecting girl whom he defiles with his blood, thus stealing her from her own people.'[2]

So he believed in 1923, when he dictated the words to Hess. And nineteen years on, talking to his court in the Wolfsschanze, his headquarters in East Prussia, he often discoursed upon comparable themes – for example, upon the fact that 'the Jew' was always on the look-out to destroy 'the natural order' by 'sleight of hand': 'The Jew introduced Christianity into the ancient world – in order to ruin it – re-opened the same breach in modern times – this time taking as his pretext the social question. It's the same sleight of hand as before. Just as Saul was changed into St Paul, Mordechai became Karl Marx ...' He had decided that 'the people that is rid of its Jews returns spontaneously to the natural order'.[3]

Already, by the middle of the war, Germans were beginning to recognize what it felt like to be on the way towards achieving natural order. For one thing, they had toothache, since most of the dentists in Germany had been deported or had gone into exile. For another, they had very few nuclear physicists left, and those who had gone were helping the Americans to pioneer nuclear weaponry. The fortunate universities of Britain and America now had their Albert Einstein, their Ernst Gombrich, their Eduard Fraenkel to adorn their faculties, thanks to the German Leader's belief that such individuals were undermining the natural order.

But most Jews in Europe had neither the money nor the opportunity to escape. Before the war, Germany was not alone in assuming the desirability of sending Jews into exile, voluntarily or otherwise. In 1937, the Polish Government approached the French and the British with a view to dispatching a million Jews either to Madagascar or to British South Africa. In 1938, the French Foreign Minister, Georges

Bonnet, reiterated the possibility of the Madagascar option to Ribbentrop, and, in 1939, Chamberlain and Roosevelt, realizing that the Jews were not wanted in Germany, or in German-occupied Austria, or the former Czechoslovakia, or in Poland, asked Mussolini whether there might be an opportunity to relocate them in Ethiopia, which the Italian dictator had brutally invaded and colonized two years previously.

Clearly, even among the higher Nazi echelons, the idea of forcing the Jews into exile was how they envisaged ridding Germany of its Jewish population. Heinrich Himmler, who, among his other titles, was the Reich's Commissar for the Strengthening of Ethnic Germandom, expressed the hope, on 15 May 1940, 'to see the term "Jew" completely eliminated through the possibility of a large-scale emigration of all Jews to Africa or to some colony'. In October 1943, addressing an elite gathering of SS officers in a toneless voice, he spoke for three hours. After two hours, he referred to one of the tasks which would distinguish the true Waffen-SS man from the lily-livered ordinary German. Every normal German, he admitted, while tolerating, or even approving, the ill-treatment of Jews, would want to make an exception in the case of Jews known to them personally. It was to be their task, in the SS, to have no such scruples. 'Most of you men know what it is like to see 100 corpses side by side, or 500 or 1,000.' Because they were men who were capable of cruelty on a stupendous scale, they were the ones who would spearhead the Final Solution – 'I am referring here to the evacuation of the Jews, the extermination of the Jewish people.'[4]

Within less than three years, the Nazis had moved from the position of wanting to send the Jews into exile to calculating a means of killing them *en masse*. It was the cover of war which allowed them to do it, and it was their conquest of so much of Eastern Europe which so enormously increased the number of their victims. Jews numbered less than 1 per cent of the population in Germany and many of these had left. In Poland, Romania, and the Ukraine, it was a different story, with millions of Jews stranded, and unable to fly to the free world.

In 1941 Goebbels proposed to Hitler that the 78,000 Jews left in Berlin be made to wear the yellow Star of David on their clothing. It was a 'scandal' that 'these parasites' were allowed to disfigure the city, and Germans must look forward to a time when Berlin could become free of the Jews altogether, when they had been forced out and 'pushed East'. 'We must approach the problem without any sentimentality. One only has to imagine what the Jews would do to us if they had the power, to know what one must do, given that we have the power.'[5] Hitler readily agreed.

The sheer energy wasted on their monstrous schemes of persecution, and eventually of mass murder, weakened the Nazi effectiveness in the war against Russia, and against the Western Allies. It also damaged the German economy. The war had caused acute labour shortages, and the murder or enforced movement of skilled Jewish workers away from their jobs left vacancies which could not be filled. The German workforce shrank during the war from

39 million to 29 million at a time when the war effort clearly required an increase of production in many vital areas.

'Our country today is overpopulated', Hitler remarked one evening in August 1942, 'and the numbers emigrating to America are incredible. How I wish we had the German-Americans with us still. In so far as there are any decent people in America, they are all of German origin.'[6] Like so many Hitler epigrams, it is a closely packed set of contradictions. Naturally, he was referring to the non-Jewish Germans who do indeed make up a large proportion of the American population. Yet there was a paradox, to put it mildly, in both deploring the over-population of Germany and wishing that the Germans in America would come back. It could be said that he had been doing his bit to decrease the population, with the gassing of the mentally ill, the driving of not only Jews but many others into voluntary exile, and the eventual slaughter of so many German Jews – not to mention the prodigious number of war casualties which came about as a result of the war he had himself instigated – the millions lost in battle, the 600,000 civilians eventually to be killed by aerial bombardment.

The Nazis nonsensically convinced themselves that the confiscation of Jewish property would solve the housing shortage. Bureaucratic rules were drawn up for the 'evacuation' of Jewish families when their houses and flats were taken away from them. They must leave the properties 'clean and tidy'. Rent and utility bills must be settled. Keys must be handed in to the local Gestapo before the victims were sent to what would almost inevitably be their deaths.

Hitler was the prime author of this policy and of all the subsequent murders. Though his inner circle enthusiastically endorsed the policy, and though there were others who worked out the gruesome schemes of slave labour, starvation, or simple massacres prior to cremation in specially designed ovens, it was Adolf Hitler who was the prime mover, and the chief architect.

By October 1941, at Hitler's specific command, Jewish emigration from the Reich was banned. The next month, mobile gas vans were used to kill Jews in Lodz in Poland and soon after that in Chelmno. Himmler's deputy, SS General Reinhard Heydrich, pioneered the use of these mobile vans (which had initially been used to exterminate over 70,000 mental patients). They were simple devices, in which the carbon monoxide, instead of passing out through an exhaust pipe, turned back into the van. Mass shootings took place all over Eastern Europe. An SS officer in the German embassy in Paris came up with the idea of using Jewish slave labour in a vast road-building scheme – Transit Route IV, a supply road running from Przemysl in the south-east of Poland via Lviv and Tarnapol and far into the Ukraine – with the road surface to be constructed from the rubble of demolished synagogues and Jewish gravestones. In the labour camps which were established all over the East, hundreds of thousands of Jews perished from starvation or disease. The ultimate horror, if comparisons between one unspeakable experience and another can meaningfully be made, was in the camps delib- erately constructed for the purpose of eliminating human beings by gassing on a huge scale. Auschwitz is the name best known to history, for it was at this Polish location that 1,100,000 people died. But there were many other places. At Treblinka, also in Poland, 900,000 died.

Throughout German-occupied Europe, the Jews were rounded up: a quarter of the Jews in France; three-quarters of the Jews in the Netherlands; Jews from Greece, and from Romania, where the local population was especially murder- ous towards them; from Bulgaria and Hungary, men, women and children were taken to their deaths. Hitler was respon- sible for the massacre of six million Jews.

When the war was over, and the mass graves were discov- ered, and the camps were liberated, the world watched the newsreels with an appalled incredulity. The mounds of chil- dren's shoes, or of false teeth, were complemented by the heaped piles of skulls and skeletons. The skeletal survivors in their striped pyjamas stared at the cameras, making those who had fought against Adolf Hitler feel that all the mayhem and bloodshed of war over the previous six years had been experienced in a righteous cause. Under the cover of a war which had in any event been bloodier and more destructive than any conflict in the history of the human race, this other evil had been perpetrated, a mass slaughter so vast in its extent and so gruesome in its metaphysical motivations that the story has been told over and over again, in films and plays and histories and works of philosophical analysis. Behind the gas chambers, the heaps of human remains, and the debased, dehumanized characters of those who operated these camps, there lay the dark story of European anti-Semitism, stretching back to the Christian belief, embedded in the Gospels, that the Jews had committed the ultimate blasphemy – deicide: the killing of the Incarnate God. No one will ever plumb the murky depths of this terrible story. But while hundreds of thousands – perhaps millions – of human beings are implicated in the guilt of it, one man stands out as the demonic maestro who made Auschwitz a possibility and thereby made almost everyone who has ever seen one of those post-war newsreels or read the story feel that new wastes of human heartlessness, new depths of mad wickedness, had been reached. That gruesome pioneer was Hitler.

TEN

1941–1945 Defeat

Hindsight makes it obvious that Hitler's blunders as a war leader made the defeat of Germany inevitable. The first big mistake was in allowing the British Expeditionary Force to escape in the Dunkirk retreat. The defeat of the Luftwaffe in the Battle of Britain made the invasion of Britain in the summer of 1940 all the harder for Hitler, but had he made the attempt, and been successful, he would have been in a much stronger position to launch his great invasion of Russia the next year. The failure to join forces with the Japanese in the Russian campaign was another catastrophic mistake, ensuring the debacle of the whole Barbarossa campaign. The massacre of the Jews, as well as dissipating energy which could have been spent on the war effort, deprived the Reich of some of its finest minds and most skilled workers. By the end of 1941, Hitler had guaranteed that he would be defeated, and it was principally the Red Army which was his nemesis.

The Battle of Stalingrad in the winter of 1942–3 was the turning point of the war. Unlike Zhukov, Montgomery or

MacArthur, Hitler was not a strategist, and he was trying to direct the fighting at Stalingrad from East Prussia, thousands of miles behind the lines, using a street-map of the city. It was at this point that Providence turned her back on him.

As if the disaster of Barbarossa was not enough, and almost as if he wanted to make his defeat an ineluctable conclusion to his violent career, Hitler had declared war on the United States of America.

The victory over the Germans, however, was not easy, nor even perhaps inevitable, not least because the Wehrmacht, the German army, was a superbly trained fighting force, with some outstanding military commanders. One of the most brilliant was Lieutenant General Erwin Rommel. He was the most esteemed general, of whatever country, during the entire war. The British felt him to be a decent man and an admirable soldier. Some thought Churchill would lose a vote of confidence in the House of Commons after the Socialist MP Nye Bevan asked the House whether anyone believed that Rommel – were he an Englishman – would have risen above the rank of sergeant. He was making the point that England was still class-bound. Rommel, a brilliant man of the people, had won fame in the First World War as a young lieutenant at the Battle of Caporetto when he captured over eighty Italian guns and 9,000 men. In the Second World War, he was the mastermind behind the Blitzkrieg idea – that is, that sudden attack was the most effective war strategy. He was largely responsible for the defeat of France, and in 1941, Hitler put Rommel in charge of the Afrika Korps where, as the legendary Desert Fox, he looked as if he was going to secure North Africa, and hence the entire Mediterranean, for the Axis. Had he done so, it would have made Churchill's plan for the invasion of Europe – through Sicily and Italy – an impossibility. The Allies would have invaded the French coast without the backup of the Eighth Army in Italy, and this would have been a risky undertaking. As D-Day in 1944 revealed, the landings were not easy and heavy losses were to be inevitable.

By 1941, Churchill had peaked as a war leader and was making blunder after blunder, with consequent enormous loss of life: the failure to wrest Greece and Crete from the Germans was only one of them. The Germans retained command of the Balkans. Belgrade was flattened by German bombs.

Rommel was able to recapture North African strongholds, such as Tobruk, taken from the Italians by the Australians. When Tobruk fell in June 1942 he took 30,000 prisoners. In the course of that summer, however, Rommel became ill and flew back to Germany, suffering from a combination of stomach and liver complaints and high blood pressure. He left the Afrika Korps in the charge of the obese General Georg Stumme. On the British side, General Montgomery had recently taken over command of the Eighth Army and defeated the Germans by a combination of tactical ingenuity and sheer force of numbers. He built up a huge force of Commonwealth soldiers – 195,000 compared to the 50,000 Germans and 54,000 Italians. With two to one superiority, he defeated Rommel, who had returned to Africa, sixty miles from Alexandria at El Alamein. The Germans fought with superb courage and determination, but they were over-whelmed by sheer numbers. Thereafter, the Eighth Army was in a position, eventually, to invade Sicily and begin the long, painful slog up Italy in appalling conditions.

Two things about Hitler manifested themselves as the war turned into the last two years of painful blood-letting. One was that the condition of his health was rapidly declining. The other was that, far from being depressed by the levels of slaughter, he positively gloried in it.

The condition of his health alone rendered him quite unsuited as the war leader of a great world power. By this stage of the war, Dr Morell was pumping Hitler with at least twenty-eight different drug-mixtures (excluding the morphia and hypnotics which were sometimes needed to calm him down). These included the proprietary narcotic 'Ultraseptyl', condemned by decent pharmacologists, as well as various fake medicines, quack stimulants and aphrodisiacs. When we use the word 'pumping', this is no less than the truth. Professor Karl Brandt, Hitler's surgeon, testified that 'Morell took more and more to treatment by injections until by the end he was doing all his work by this method. For instance, he would give large doses of sulphonamides for slight colds, and gave them to everyone at Hitler's headquarters. Morell and I had many disputes about this. Morell then took to giving injections that had dextrose, hormones, vitamins, etc. So that the patient immediately felt better; and this type of treatment seemed to impress Hitler. Whenever he felt a cold coming on, he would have three to six injections daily, and thus prevent any real development of the infection. Therapeutically this was satisfactory. Then Morell used it as a prophylactic. If Hitler had to deliver a speech on a cold or rainy day, he would have injections the day before, the day of the speech and the day after. The normal resistance of the body was thus replaced by an artificial medium. When the war began, Hitler thought himself indispensable, and throughout the war he received almost continual injections. During the last two years he was injected daily. When I asked Dr Morell to name the drugs employed, he refused. Hitler depended more and more on these injections; his dependence became very obvious during the last year.'[1]

From 1943 onwards, Hitler, though scarcely in his mid-fifties, had many of the characteristics of a sick old man. He could no longer read without spectacles. His extremities trembled, especially the left arm and the left leg. His left foot dragged along the ground. He stooped. Some doctors believe that he had developed Parkinson's disease. Others have attributed the tremors to hysterical origins. After the Battle of Stalingrad in 1942–3, Hitler only made two major public speeches. He led an increasingly eremitic existence, travelling through Germany with the train-carriage blinds down. Hans Fallada's haunting novel *Jeder Stirbt für Sich Allein*, translated as *Alone in Berlin*, tells of a late middle-aged couple's feeling of total disillusionment with Hitler after their son is killed during the invasion of France. They are not especially political. They cannot join up with a resistance movement. But in their desperation they take to leaving postcards, dotted around Berlin – in stair-wells, on pavements and walls – denouncing the regime. There is an obvious authenticity in Fallada's depiction of how ruthlessly (and how inefficiently) the secret police attempt to discover who has been placing these damaging attacks on the great Leader. Fallada's record, by a man who lived through those terrible years, shows how difficult even minimal resistance was in Germany. The decision, long before the Nazis came to power, to build up an unbending party machine, with a system of snooping, bullying and relentless interference in the lives of others, meant that, however stupid the individual officers, a system was in place which made resistance extremely hard.

Pastor Bonhoeffer, one of the most articulate of the anti-Nazi voices since the rise of the Third Reich, tried to send word to his friend in England, George Bell, Bishop of Chichester, that there was indeed a resistance movement in Germany, that not all Germans supported the insane Hitler or his repellent life-view. For this reason, Bell vociferously opposed the carpet bombing of German cities and urged upon Churchill and his government a policy which sought to make peace with the enlightened part of Germany, rather than punish a whole country for the sins of the Nazis. His wish for a negotiated peace rather than unconditional surrender earned Bell much vilification in Britain which, like the rest of the world, was gripped with war fever.

It was true that there was resistance in Germany, but it lacked organization and leadership. In 1943, Sophie Scholl, a

Munich student, together with her brother and his friends, distributed anti-Nazi leaflets on the campus of the university. She, her brother and another student were all beheaded in February 1943. At the same time, her father was in prison for making an uncomplimentary remark about Hitler which had been repeated to a colleague at work.

There were Germans in plenty who had always detested National Socialism. And by the turning-point of the war, and the disastrous Russian campaign, there were many who had previously believed in Hitler who were now disillusioned, aware that he had lied to his people about wanting peace, and was insatiable in his bloodlust. But the recognition that Germany was lost until it got rid of Hitler and the Nazis did not make it easier to achieve the desired goal.

Sophie Scholl was a Christian pacifist. Dietrich Bonhoeffer was a complicated, highly intelligent Lutheran, who had once considered pacifism a *sine qua non* of Christianity, but who, in his book *Ethics*, worked out what he conceived as the essential self-indulgence of such a position. To say that one would never kill, while hoping that Hitler would somehow be removed from the scene, was to ask other people to do one's dirty work. Bonhoeffer (whose psychiatrist father, it will be remembered, had given it as his opinion that Hitler was insane) came to believe that it was a Christian as well as his moral duty to support the assassination of the Leader.

Bonhoeffer worked for the Abwehr, the German army's intelligence organization, many of whose members were involved with a series of conspiracies throughout 1943 to assassinate Hitler. When the Gestapo became aware of this, Dietrich Bonhoeffer was imprisoned. He was eventually hanged with piano wire for his distant connection to the most famous conspiracy of all, and the one which stood the greatest chance of succeeding, that of the aristocratic Colonel Claus Schenk von Stauffenberg in July 1944.

In June of that year, the Western Allies, with terrible loss of life on all sides, had accomplished the invasion of northern France on the beaches of Normandy. Germany was now faced with the combined might of the British and American armies and air forces in the west. To the east, the Red Army, with its apparently limitless numbers and its apparently inexhaustible hardware, had emerged victorious from the Barbarossa campaign and was fighting hard on the Eastern Front.

A crisis had been reached and Germany was faced with an unavoidable defeat. A group of senior army officers, many of whom were old Prussian nobility, felt that the time had obviously come to stage a coup d'état, and to negotiate some kind of dignified peace with the British, Russians and Americans. On 17 June, Hitler, after repeatedly unsuccessful attempts to persuade him to come near the theatre of war, finally agreed to meet Rommel and Field Marshal Gerd von Rundstedt in Margival, north of Soissons. Only four years before, it had been the headquarters set up for the invasion of England. Now the generals were trying to make their Leader see that the game was up. The officers all stood while the Leader, pale, sleepless, agitated, sat hunched on a stool, and played with his spectacles or fumbled with pencils with shaking hands. Hitler was clearly in no mood to face reality. He spoke of the invincible secret 'V' weapons and the innumerable turbo-jet fighters which would appear in the skies and bring England to her knees. Rommel tried to tell him that the time had come to bring the war to an end. 'Don't you worry about the continuance of the war', Hitler told him, 'but about your invasion front.' Meanwhile, as everyone in the room knew, the Allies had landed a million men and half a million tons of material in France.

Hitler's next move was to sack Rundstedt and replace him with Field Marshal Günther von Kluge. It was at this point that Stauffenberg, who had returned from the Eastern Front and seen the successes inflicted on German troops by the Red Army, decided upon his assassination attempt. He made two visits to the Berghof in Berchtesgaden but on each occasion he had held back from planting a bomb because Göring and Himmler, who had promised to be present, had failed to show. Stauffenberg hoped to take out not merely Hitler but these two fellow-criminals if it were at all possible.

On 20 July the Leader's headquarters were moved from Berchtesgaden to Rastenburg in East Prussia – the settlement known as the Wolf's Lair. At the last minute, the venue for the military conference was changed, from one army hut to another. Stauffenberg, who had almost been surprised by fellow-officers, with pliers and wires actually in his hand, hastily planted a bomb, concealed in a briefcase, under the map table where the Leader was due to outline his latest catastrophic plans. It turned out to be a marble-topped table.

Stauffenberg withdrew to a different part of the barracks, and after the huge, highly satisfying explosion, he assumed that he had at last been successful in achieving the end for which all sane Germans, and indeed men and women throughout the world, had been yearning: Hitler's death. Following the explosion came the smoke. Wood and paper were hurled into the air. Stauffenberg left the barracks hastily and flew to Berlin, telling his friends that the Leader was no more.

He was not correct. As so often happened in Hitler's life, there was a strong element of farce, unrecognized as such – of course – by the central participants. The Leader staggered out of the smoke and rubble alive. His trousers were in tatters. He afterwards seemed to regard these trousers as something in the order of a sacred relic, holding them up as evidence that Providence, or whatever cruel god in whom he half-believed, had yet again spared him to continue inflicting unhappiness on everyone else on the planet. Mussolini sent a message saying that this was 'a sign from Heaven'.

For the first half of the day after the explosion, Hitler was in a state of miraculous calm, quietly sucking various coloured lozenges supplied by Dr Morell. Then, towards 5 p.m. in the afternoon, back in the Leader's bunker, the raving mania surfaced. A group had assembled around him, and they were beginning to bicker among themselves. Admiral Dönitz said it revealed the treachery of the army. Göring said it betrayed the pitiful foreign policy of the Reich. Göring took offence at Dönitz's implied attack on the Air Force. Ribbentrop took offence at the attack on his Foreign Ministry.

Suddenly, through their bickering voices there broke the sound of Hitler shouting. It was one of his most unrestrained pieces of anger. Those responsible for trying to defy Providence would be punished. So would their wives. So would their children. As he bayed and yelled, calling for deaths and more deaths, white-clad SS servants moved about serving tea and refilling china cups.

The Leader announced his intention of speaking to the German people at once. In fact, he did not reach the radio microphones until 1 a.m., but there must have been many who stayed up to hear the rasping, violent tones as he addressed them –

> German racial comrades! I do not know how many times an assassination attempt against me has been planned and carried out. If I speak to you today I do so for two reasons: first so that you may hear my voice and know that I myself am uninjured and well. Secondly so that you may also learn the details about a crime that has not its like in German history.[2]

Having named Stauffenberg as the instigator of the treason, and assured the public that those involved in the plot were a 'ridiculously small' number of officers, he promised that 'we will settle accounts the way we National Socialists are accustomed to settle them'.

This was a promise which he found easy to keep. The arrests and executions were still going on in April 1945, when the war was ending. Anyone suspected of being implicated was hauled before a military tribunal. Some 5,000 people were killed for being involved with the plot. They were allowed no chance to plead, no lawyers, no visits from chaplains or religious consolations of any kind before their deaths. 'I want them to be hanged, strung up like butchered cattle', Hitler said. And Himmler in a speech in August promised, inaccurately, that 'the family of Count von Stauffenberg will be wiped out down to the last member'.[3]

The plot was crushed but it crushed Hitler psychologically. He could no longer trust anyone, even his dearest one. Secretaries overheard him say crossly to his German Shepherd dog, 'Look me in the eyes, Blondi. Are you also a traitor like the generals of my staff?'[4]

Only Rommel was spared the gallows. General Wilhelm Burgdorf was sent to the Desert Fox with a revolver and a cyanide capsule. He was informed that if he committed suicide there would be no publicity and no reprisals on his family. This was cynical, not merciful. A public trial of Rommel would have revealed the extent of distrust of Hitler felt by the senior military. Rommel did his Führer a great favour by committing suicide.

During the last months of 1944, the Americans advanced almost to the German border. Though her allies and friends – Vichy France, Finland, Bulgaria, Romania – had by now capitulated to the Anglo-American or Soviet attacks, Germany fought on. About 1.2 million Germans died on the Western Front during this period. When General Alfred Jodl

(Chief of Operations Staff of the German High Command) showed Hitler the map of where they were taking the heaviest pounding, in the hilly area between Luxembourg and Belgium, Hitler stabbed at the paper. 'I have made a momentous decision. I am taking the offensive. Here, out of the Ardennes.'

It was a bold stroke. Some 250,000 German troops were moved to the line of departure. The battle raged through late November and December in heavy snows, wild winds and biting sleet. They managed to give the Americans a run for their money but in the event, they could not cross the River Meuse, and by the beginning of 1945 it was evident that General Eisenhower's troops, badly demoralized as they were, had the advantage over the Germans. Hitler was furious and said that the campaign had only failed because his instructions had not been carried out to the letter. But the truth was, as Jodl put it to the screaming Hitler, 'My Leader, we cannot force the Meuse.' Over 75,000 men had been killed in what the Americans, not troubling to acquaint themselves with any of the place-names of the Ardennes forests, called simply the Battle of the Bulge.

As the Americans under the command of General George S. Patton pressed on to victory, Hitler gave a New Year broadcast. Germany, he predicted, would rise like a phoenix from its ruined cities and go on to victory.

ELEVEN

The Bunker

During a nocturnal discussion with Himmler in 1941, Hitler once expressed his ambition to make Berlin the capital of the world. 'What is ugly in Berlin we shall suppress. Nothing will be too good for the beautification of Berlin. When one enters the Reich Chancellery, one should have the feeling that one is visiting the Master of the World. One will arrive there along long avenues containing the Triumphal Arch, the Pantheon of the Army, the Square of the People – things to take your breath away! It is only thus that we shall succeed in eclipsing our only rival in the world, Rome. Let it be built on such a scale that St Peter's and its Square will seem like toys in comparison!'[1]

Far from rebuilding Berlin on this majestic scale, Hitler was to end his days huddled beneath it in a bunker, as Russian field guns pounded the ruins left by the aerial raids of British and American bombers. Hitler's war left Berlin, and most other German cities, a smouldering heap of rubble.

Hitler returned to Berlin from East Prussia in November 1944 and he would never leave it again. By the time he came back, the bombing of the city had escalated to nightmare proportions. In fact, Berlin was to suffer bombardment on a scale which few cities or conurbations could ever expect to survive. The new leader of British Bomber Command, Arthur Harris, told the head of the Royal Air Force, Charles Portal, 'It is my firm belief that we are on the verge of a final show-down.' That had been in August 1943. On 3 November of the same year he had told Churchill, 'We can wreck Berlin from end to end if the US Air Force will come in on it.' More bombs were dropped on Berlin in the following year than fell on the whole of Britain during the entire war: 33,390 tons. By March 1944, 1.5 million Berliners were homeless. About 52,000 civilians were killed by aerial bombing. By the end of the war, Harris had ordered 14,562 sorties over the city and the Americans had indeed 'come in on it'. Even when it was quite obvious that the bombing was not working, Harris continued to pound the city.

The Berliners showed astounding resilience. Their natural obedience manifested itself in the fact that even when the Treasury offices were flattened, Berliners continued to pay their taxes, some clambering over the ruins of the Treasury to see if they could find an official to whom they could offer their dues.[2] This paralleled the remarkable behaviour of the villagers of Baden in 1945 after they had been occupied by the Americans and the Gestapo had fled to a nearby mountain retreat; the villagers would still stagger up the mountain for the chance to inform the Gestapo of their neighbours' defeat-ist attitude.[3] 'We Germans have that marvellous source of strength – the sense of duty – which other peoples do not possess', as Hitler himself had remarked in happier days.[4]

In Berlin, red-eyed, pale, hungry people continued to trudge to work every day after a night of raids and to work for twelve hours in factories and offices. A typical Berliner was Frau Ursula Meyer-Semlies: 'Goebbels did say we are sitting in a moving train and no one can get out … Can one answer it in one's conscience, for one's children, for the future, simply to "throw the rifle into the cornfield"? No we have to keep going until the end.'[5] The truth is that while there was a widespread feeling that Hitler and the Nazis had led Germany to its ruin, there was also a sense, among others, that 'the Fatherland fights on', and that the Leader would, in spite of everything, rise up like a magician to save them. They had no choice and they behaved with courage.

Hitler lived at first in the Chancellery and then, when the bombing grew too much, he retired to his underground bunker with Blondi, the German Shepherd bitch given to him by his private secretary, Martin Bormann, in 1942 to take his mind off the failure of the Russian campaign. Blondi – unless you count the Leader's girlfriend Eva Braun – was Hitler's last attachment. Little Fuchsl, the English terrier, had consoled him in the trenches. Prinz, Muckl and Wolf, his three German Shepherds, were now presumably either dead, or living out an extreme old age in Berchtesgaden. 'I should feel like a traitor if I became attached to a dog of any other breed. What extraordinary animals they are! Lively, loyal, bold, courageous and handsome.' And, he could have added, more obedient than people, with all their complexities of thought and language. Upon Blondi, he lavished the attention and love which only the dog-lover can bestow, presumably loving the bad breath, the slobbering, the ever-present possibility of snarling violence and the hyper-energy of the species. But above all, perhaps, the slavishness.

Eva Braun, in spite of being Hitler's mistress, did possess a mind of her own; she liked to smoke cigarettes, despite the Leader's abhorrence of the habit. Eva hated Blondi, and would kick her under the table. It is not surprising, since Hitler, in common with many dog-lovers, was incapable of showing the same affection for any human being such as that which poured out of him when feeding, or stroking, or staring into the eyes of this smelly near-cousin of the wolf.

In these early months of 1945, it was clear to everyone except the deranged Leader that the Germans had lost the war. The war which had begun to rescue Eastern Europe from the hands of two repressive tyrannies – Nazi Germany and Soviet Russia – was about to be won by Soviet Russia. Not caring how many of his own men perished in the attempt, Stalin pressed his Red Army onwards to conquer Berlin while the American forces under General Patton slowly lumbered through the Ruhr.

On both its borders, Germany was now overwhelmed. Berlin had become a surreal inferno, with almost 3 million of its inhabitants trapped in the cellars of the vast flak towers (anti-aircraft emplacements) or in bunkers or, if their homes possessed cellars, underground at home. Hitler followed suit by retreating to his elaborately constructed complex of tunnels and rooms beneath the Chancellery and the other government buildings. He emerged into Berlin only twice after January 1945 – once to attend a meeting of Gauleiters on the outskirts of the city, and once to visit General Theodor Busse to discuss the by now hopeless defence of the River Oder. On both occasions, the blinds of the car were kept firmly closed. He did not wish to set eyes upon the ruin he had created. He never once visited a bomb-site.

When his narcotic-fuelled moods in the Bunker allowed him to be happy, he would continue to discuss the rebuilding of Berlin with Speer. He also possessed a huge architectural model of Linz, the scene of his youth, where he and Kubizek had first heard Wagner's *Rienzi* and where 'it' had all begun. Fully uniformed, Hitler would sit beside this fantasy-version of Linz staring admiringly at the miniature wooden streets and towers. It worried him that the dream tower was a little too tall. 'It must not eclipse the spire of the cathedral at Ulm', he told anyone who would listen. 'In the tower I want a carillon to play – not every day but on special days – a theme from Bruckner's Fourth – the Romantic symphony.' He had come to love Bruckner more and more, especially the Seventh Symphony. 'Brahms was praised to the heavens by Jewry, a creature of salons, a theatrical figure with his flowing hair and beard and his hands poised above the keyboard. Bruckner, on the other hand, a shrunken little man, would probably have been too shy to play in such society.'[6]

The architectural dreams were symptomatic of the fact that Hitler was now totally insane, removed from reality. As the bunker rocked with explosions, caused by the guns, Hitler telephoned General Karl Koller to complain of the noise, and told him to stop the firing. He refused to believe Koller when told that these were Russian guns that were now within range of the city centre.

When the noise over the roof became too much, or when the true progress of the war was brought to the Leader's attention, he would react, as he had reacted to so much in life during the last few years, with outbursts of petulant and uncontrollable rage. At the end of April Hitler gave orders that the 950 bridges in Berlin all be destroyed, which would have cut off all electricity and supplies from the hundreds of thousands of people still trapped in the centre. Albert Speer, the architect who received the order, disobeyed it. Speer, who had done so much to promote Hitler and his myth, designing the great rallies at Nuremberg and encouraging Hitler in his megalomaniac dreams, now began to think of ways of killing him, and the other occupants of the bunker, by feeding poison gas through a ventilator shaft. When he investigated the possibilities of this scheme he discovered that the Leader, paranoid about his own experience of being gassed during the previous war, had blocked up the shaft with a concrete chimney breast.

Everyone trapped in that bunker – Blondi, the secretaries, the valet, the Leader, Eva Braun, the dwarfish Goebbels, his tragically majestic wife and their six children – were now obliged to see the grisly drama to its end. In the carpeted study with its maps and atlases, and its portrait of Frederick the Great hanging on the wall, Dr Goebbels would read aloud to the Leader, when the thunder of gunfire permitted it, from the *Life of Frederick the Great* by the unmatchable Scottish historian-prophet Thomas Carlyle. How much Carlyle, with his boundless capacity for scorn and his humorous contempt for any kind of pretension, would have despised these two men. Goebbels read the scene where Frederick's arch-enemy, the Russian Empress Elizabeth, died in the 'Miracle of the House of Brandenburg', allowing the Prussians to snatch victory from the jaws of defeat. History seemed to repeat itself when President Roosevelt died on 12 April. It was Hitler's Brandenburg miracle and for a day or two he was exultant.

But when Hitler's fifty-sixth birthday occurred, on 20 April, the Allies had not behaved as the Russians had behaved in Carlyle's book. They had not sued for peace and conceded a German triumph. Goebbels broadcast to the world by radio his customary annual eulogy, while underground, as the roof and walls shook with bombardment, the quivering and furious Hitler exclaimed, 'You will see – the Russians are about to suffer the bloodiest defeat of their history at the gates of Berlin.' By now over 52,000 Berliners had been killed by the air raids alone and it was only a matter of days before the Red Army conquered their capital.

Göring sent him a telegram asking if it was his wish that he, Göring, should take over as Leader in the event of Berlin being surrounded. He proposed making peace with the enemy. This act of impertinent treachery was greeted by paroxysms of anger on Hitler's part. Then, on 28 April, Hitler heard the news that even the faithful Himmler had been in conversation with the Swedish diplomat Count Bernadotte to broker a peace between Germany and her enemies. He ordered that Himmler should be stripped of all his titles and arrested.

But by then he knew that the end had come. A local magistrate, serving in a nearby militia unit, with the curiously appropriate name of Walter Wagner, was brought to the bunker to marry the Leader to Eva Braun. When she signed the register, Eva initially began to write her maiden name and then corrected the B to an H as she realized she was now called Frau Hitler.

She was not to have this privilege for long. On 28 April, Mussolini and his mistress Clara Petacci had been captured by the Italian Communists in the small northern hamlet of Mezzagra, and shot. They took the bodies to Milan, where they were strung upside down. A baying mob pulled down the dead Clara's knickers.

Hitler was determined that he and Eva should provide no such spectacle for the mob. Nor would he allow the Russians to take him to Moscow for a 'show trial staged by Jews'. He charged his manservant, Heinz Linge, his chauffeur, Erich Kempka, and his pilot, Hans Baur, with the task of incinerating the bodies of himself and his wife. After lunch on 30 April, he took leave of his staff.

Blondi had been the first to die. Hitler tested a cyanide capsule on her to see that it would work. Eva also took poison. Accounts differ as to whether Hitler died by also taking poison or whether he died of a gunshot. The SS guards outside his room testified that they heard a single shot. When they went in, they found Eva dead and the Leader, also dead, hunched beside her, his face covered with blood.

Kempka and Bormann carried the bodies outside and, with Russian shells splintering the concrete about their ears, they soused the corpses with petrol. Goebbels was standing by with a box of matches at the ready. That evening they did their best to put the charred, but not completely incinerated, remains into a shell hole and cover it with earth.

Goebbels next attempted to get hold of the Russians and to negotiate a separate peace, cutting out the British and the Americans. It came to nothing, and so the next day there followed the gruesome murder of all six of his children – his wife Magda crunching their jaws over cyanide capsules. Although she had made them drowsy with drugged cocoa, some force was needed to murder her daughter Helga. Next followed the suicides of Magda and Joseph Goebbels themselves.

On 1 May, Radio Hamburg announced that Hitler was dead. 'He died for Germany in his command post at the Reich Chancellery, fighting to his last breath against Bolshevism.'[7]

A week later, General Jodl signed an act of surrender in Eisenhower's war room at Reims. Stalin refused to accept this since it was not made in the presence of the Russians. The next day, Field Marshal Keitel, head of the German Armed

Forces, was flown to Tempelhof Airport and, in one of the few buildings in Berlin left standing, he made an act of unconditional surrender to Marshal Zhukov and representatives of the French, the British and the Americans. But everyone knew that, as the Radio Hamburg broadcast had said, the true battle had been against Communist Russia, and that Stalin was the true victor of the war.

TWELVE

Final Verdict

Hitler was the Enlightenment's cloven hoof. From the time of Voltaire, it had been assumed by enlightened Europeans that if only the human race could throw off the outmoded thought-processes of religion and espouse a scientific outlook, the human race would become free. Thomas Carlyle, himself a child of the Enlightenment, and a religious doubter, knew that this was too simple a reading of the past. Reviewing the eighteenth century, he saw the great sceptic David Hume as only half a man. Even when belief in a personal God has been discarded, there remained, as Immanuel Kant knew, a reverence for the starry heavens above us and the moral law within. An attempt to forget these primary truths meant that the human race would always come unstuck. And that, surely, is what Carlyle would have thought of the Hitler story – that it exemplified more than anything else the futility of the 'modern' or 'scientific' outlook on life.

Richard Wagner is viewed with suspicion by many who see him as a forerunner of his admirer Adolf Hitler. Some of the same taint by association clings to Thomas Carlyle, that witty philosopher-historian, whose immense biography *Frederick the Great* beguiled some of Hitler's last hours. But Carlyle was no Fascist and he can survive the disapproval of those who have not even taken the trouble to read him.

You can see, however, why they – the non-Carlyle readers – believe him to have been one of the early exponents of that dark form of political cynicism. In his book *Heroes and Hero-Worship*, Carlyle saw history as punctuated by the arrival of these Great Men. 'The Great Man was always as lightning out of Heaven; the rest of men waited for him like fuel, and then they too would flame.' The heroes he chose included Mahomet, and Dante and Oliver Cromwell, all serious beings, who had an intense awareness of mankind's moral imperatives.

His last hero is Napoleon, whom he imagined sitting in exile on the island of St Helena unable to understand why he did not win. 'France is great, and all-great; and, at bottom, he is France. England itself, he says, is by Nature only an append-age of France ... So it was by Nature, by Napoleon-Nature; and yet look how in fact – HERE AM I! He cannot under-stand it; inconceivable that the reality has not corresponded to his programme of it.'[1]

What Carlyle concluded at the end of his surveys of 'Heroes' was that Napoleon had gone too far, that Napoleon-Nature was not the same as real Nature, and that there had been a moral fittingness about his ultimate defeat. What can be said of Napoleon can be said with infinitely more vigour of Hitler. The German dictator was not overcome ultimately because he defied Churchill, or defied the Red Army, but because he defied reality itself.

Hitler suffered just as strongly, to the very end, from a Napoleonic feeling of bafflement that things had not gone his way. 'I am beginning to doubt whether the German people is worthy of my great ideals',[2] was one of Hitler's ways of describing the difference between his plans for the world, and the way it failed to conform to them.

Speer believed that Hitler was 'one of those inexplicable historical phenomena which emerge at rare intervals among mankind. His person determined the fate of the nation. He alone placed it and kept it on the path which has led it to this dreadful ending. The nation was spellbound by him as a people has rarely been in the whole of history.'[3]

There is plenty of evidence for the spellbinding nature of Hitler the public orator, Hitler the great national Leader in his heyday. Ever since his death, humanity has been trying to make sense of it. Why? Why him? Why the Germans?

There is no one answer to the questions which arise from this bloody and horrible period of European history. For some, there will be a Hegelian or Marxist inevitability about the rise of National Socialism because of the appalling economic situation at the end of the First World War. Others, seeking among the gloomy Rhine-waters of Wagnerian music, the Satanic risks of the Faust legend, the fantastical cruelties of the Brothers Grimm or the weirder landscapes of Caspar David Friedrich, will try to suggest that Hitler trod in a discernible succession to a whole sinister Germanic tradition, just as they will try to find in his anti-Jewish ravings an ancestry in the sermons of Martin Luther.

In the end, Hitler is a mystery who cannot be plumbed, whether you use the tool of the economist, the political analyst or the psychiatrist. But two things are perhaps worth saying in conclusion. They are apparently contradictory things. Perhaps Hegel would think them a thesis and an antithesis. They are that Hitler was both very ordinary and completely extraordinary.

He was ordinary in the things he believed and in most of the things he believed he was a pioneer of the modern age. This is something which most people find extremely hard to stomach. They want to make him into a Demon King. Ever since he died by his own hand in the bunker, the civilized world has been on the run from his dangerous ideas. His belief that race 'explained' everything – one of the only 'old-fashioned' beliefs in the Hitlerian creed – has been replaced by the belief, now all but universal throughout the civilized world, that discriminating between peoples on racial grounds is a wickedness. Yet one of Dietrich Bonhoeffer's reasons for returning to Germany, where he intuitively knew that he would die a martyr's death, was because, when living in New York where he could have stayed as an academic, he went with a friend to a restaurant and was not served because the friend was black. It is easy to treat history as a pantomime with heroes and villains, and to heap all our guilt about our own beliefs, or those of our grandparents, on to a few maniacs strutting about with swastikas on their arms. But the truth is that Hitler, in his racial discrimination, was simply being normal. The United States and the British Empire were both racist through and through. Nor, even, did Hitler's anti-Jewish policy figure in the Western powers' reason for going to war with him.

Because we still regard him as the Demon King of history we think that if we say the opposite of what Hitler said, we shall somehow be living a better life. Hitler was a racist, so we shall be anti-racist. Hitler made homosexuals wear pink triangles, so we shall have gay marriages. Hitler was the ultimately Incorrect Person, so we shall invent Political Correctness, a system of thought which is in fact dominated by the unmentioned memory of Hitler and by being his opposite in all things, things to purge his baleful influence from the earth.

Yet in other ways, Hitler's commonplace beliefs have been less easy to shake off. He was convinced that the twentieth century was somehow different from all previous centuries, that the human race had come of age, that, having thrown off the shackles of religion, humanity was now different. 'The man of today, who is formed by the disciplines of science, has ceased taking the teaching of religion very seriously' ... 'Christianity is the worst of regressions that mankind can ever have undergone ... Since the age of fourteen I have felt liberated from the superstition that the priests used to teach ... We can be grateful to Providence which causes us to live today rather than three hundred years ago. At every street corner in those days there was a blazing stake. What a debt we owe to the men who had the courage to rebel against lies and intolerance ...'⁴

It was clear from *Table Talk* that, just as he believed he had achieved a bloodless revolution in Germany, so, in some strange way, National Socialism was the natural consequence of the Enlightenment. He believed in a crude Darwinism as do nearly all scientists today, and as do almost all 'sensible' sociologists, political commentators and journalistic wise-acres. He thought that humanity in its history was to be explained by the idea of struggle, by the survival of the fittest, by the stronger species overcoming the weaker. Unlike the Darwinians of today, Hitler merely took this belief to its logical conclusion.

Hitler's crude belief in science fed his unhesitating belief in modernity. He abolished the old black-letter Gothic type-face in which Germans had been producing books since they invented printing, and replaced it with a typeface in conformity with the rest of the Western world. He liked the idea of every family possessing a car. He built a system of motorways all over Germany. The mechanized age was one which he assumed to be good. In this respect, Hitler was like almost every politician of influence since. When Tony Blair became Prime Minister of Great Britain and Northern Ireland, he called for every child in every British primary school to be given a laptop computer. He was echoing, almost exactly, Hitler's view – 'I find it a real absurdity that even today a typewriter costs several hundred marks. One can't imagine the time wasted daily in deciphering everybody's scribbles. Why not give lessons in typewriting at primary school? Instead of religious instruction, for example.'[5]

Hitler's zest for the modern, his belief that humanity would become more reasonable when it had cast off the shackles of the past – olde-tyme handwriting, religion, and so forth – and embraced science and modern roads, was a belief shared with almost all forward-thinking people at the time, and it continues to be the underlying belief-system of the liberal intelligentsia who control the West. His belief led directly to genocide and devastating war. At the same time, he believed himself to be enlightened and forward-looking, non-smoking, vegetarian, opposed to hunting, in favour of abortion and euthanasia.

Have we asked ourselves the right questions about Hitler's 'normal' and 'ordinary' beliefs? By eliminating some of his more grotesque prejudices from our moral vocabulary, have we really cast off his legacy? Do not the politicians in today's Western world, when they wish to impose their values on some other nation or group of peoples, still feel themselves entitled to employ war as the ultimate weapon? Far from having cast off Hitler's legacy, many of the world's politicians, and especially those who consider themselves most enlightened, are in fact his heirs. For that reason, we will perhaps always be compelled to think about his life – and the chilling fact that in all his world-outlook and his views, Hitler was an embodiment, albeit an exaggerated embodiment, of the beliefs of the average modern person. Moreover, in the choreography of modern life, with our love of spectacularly large football stadia, pop festivals and open-air religious celebrations, are we quite sure that we are not displaying a collective, subconscious re-enactment for the Nuremberg Rallies? The modern Olympic Games, for example, are modelled on the Berlin Games of 1936. The Olympic torch was a Nazi invention.

There is, of course, another side to all this – the Hegelian antithesis to that thesis. And this is Hitler's extraordinariness. The man was a prodigy. He was, moreover, a prodigy who kept his extraordinary gifts in reserve. For the first thirty years of life, no one could possibly have guessed that this moody, feckless, shy, pale 'artist' would exercise any influence whatsoever upon the people around him, let alone upon the destiny of the human race. Until he was twenty-five, he had done almost nothing with his life except to master a certain level of skill as an architectural draughtsman and water-colourist and to listen to Wagner's operas with an obsessive attention. There followed the World War in which he believed himself to have been a heroic soldier of exceptional valour. His superiors saw him rather as a reliable messenger-boy, an underling. Even at the end of the war when so many had been killed and second- and third-rate men were needed to fill their shoes, Hitler's commanding officers still hesitated to promote him to the rank of lance-corporal, because he so obviously lacked 'leadership qualities'.

Yet, in those months after the war, when he translated his inner dreams and prejudices into spoken rhetoric, he was able to hold audiences in the palm of his hand. And, with studied seductive skill and strong political instincts, he was able, within four years, to take over the shell of a small political unit, the NSDAP, and to hold ever-greater numbers spellbound, to become the voice of the radical Right in Germany, the man whom it seemed right to call the Leader.

This story is a prodigy. He was able to do so much damage, first in Germany, and then in the rest of the world, because, as well as being an ordinary little man with the most commonplace, boringly modern outlook, he was also a species of magician. He was, as his wise critic called him, not the Leader (*Führer*) but the Seducer (*Verführer*). While the commonplace, ordinary side of Hitler insisted that the human race had come of age, that it was now led by reason not mumbo-jumbo, that it was rational and scientific, the extraordinary Hitler, the Mage-Hitler, the Wizard Hitler, demonstrated the exact opposite to be the case. His career showed that human beings in crowds behave as irrationally in modern times as they did in the Dark Ages – possibly more irrationally, since the techniques of modern broadcasting, lighting, film and propaganda can appeal to the darker depths of our chaotic souls more immediately than an old village seer or hell-fire preacher could ever hope to do. Hitler's career proved that human nature was actually as chaotic, as easily led, as superstitious, as passionate as the characters in the wilder of Dostoyevsky's novels or as the tormented mythological beings in Wagner's operas. Hitler demonstrated with the most terrifying skill that humanity can be seduced without much difficulty into acts of collective insanity. A man whose published work openly proposed the invasion of Russia and the gassing of the Jews as a solution to his country's difficulties became not merely the Leader, but the hero and Saviour of a European country which, within a little over a year of his becoming Chancellor, voted enthusiastically for him to become their absolute dictator.

So it is that we can never finish reading the story of his life without a sense of unease. Does our present world contain a Hitler? Maybe not in Linz, maybe not in the dosshouses of Vienna, but does there lurk somewhere, living at present a life of obscurity, a human being somewhere on our planet, who possesses the arcane and sinister gift, when the right historical moment arises, of once more leading the masses to frenzied acts of mutual destruction? The poet's old question remains –

What rough beast, its hour come round at last,
Slouches towards Bethlehem to be born?

NOTES

Chapter 1: 'In that Hour it Began'

1 W. M. Thackeray, *Vanity Fair*, chapter XVII
2 Adolf Hitler, *Mein Kampf* (Munich, 1938) p.1.
3 Ian Kershaw, *Hitler 1889–1936: Hubris* (London, 1998) p.74.
4 *Guardian*, 20 August 2010.
5 *Independent*, 21 October 2010.
6 Hitler, *Mein Kampf*, p.220.
7 *Ibid.*, p.223.

Chapter 2: 'Our Leader'

1 John Toland, *Adolf Hitler* (New York, 1976) p.85.
2 Hitler, *Mein Kampf*, p.116.
3 *Ibid.*, p.98.
4 *Ibid.*, p.405.
5 *Ibid.*, p.308.
6 *Ibid.*, p.406.
7 *Ibid.*, p.406.

8 Kershaw, *Hubris*, p.159.

9 Quoted in Alan Bullock, *Hitler: A Study in Tyranny* (New York, 1952) p.75.

10 Joachim Fest, *Hitler* (London, 1974) p.240.

Chapter 3: 1921–1923 My Struggle

1 Bullock, *Hitler*, p.90.

2 Andrew Roberts, *Holy Fox: A Biography of Lord Halifax* (London, 1991) p.73.

3 Ernst Hanfstaengl, quoted in Bullock, *Hitler*, p.108.

4 Quoted in Toland, *Adolf Hitler*, p.213.

5 Quoted in Fest, *Hitler*, p.192.

6 *Ibid.*, p.192.

7 *Ibid.*, p.192.

8 Toland, *Adolf Hitler*, p.267.

Chapter 4: 1923–1929 The Politics of Catastrophe

1 Toland, *Adolf Hitler*, p.283.

2 Fest, *Hitler*, pp.159–60.

3 Kershaw, *Hubris*, p.212; Fest, *Hitler*, p.111.

4 Kershaw, *Hubris*, p.236.

5 Quoted in *ibid.*, p.196.

6 Fest, *Hitler*, p.72.

7 *Ibid.*, p.243.

8 *Ibid.*, p.133.

9 Kershaw, *Hubris*, p.188.

10 Friedrich Reck-Melleczewen, *Diary of a Man in Despair* (London, 1997) p.24.

11 Hitler, *Table Talk 1941–1944* (New York, 1953) p.165.

12 The rhyme continues 'Goering has two but very small; Himmler has something sim'lar, But poor old Go-balls has no-balls at all.'

13 Kershaw, *Hubris*, p.293.

14 *Ibid.*, p.310

15 *Ibid.*, p.318.

Chapter 5: 1929–1933 A Simple Cowherd can become a Cardinal'

1 *Table Talk*, p.322.

2 *Ibid.*, p.189.

3 *Ibid.*, p.91.

4 *Ibid.*, p.101.

5 Toland, *Adolf Hitler*, p.553.

6 Quoted in *ibid.*, p.553.

7 Quoted in *ibid.*, pp.352–53.

8 Kershaw, *Hubris*, p.367.

9 *Ibid.*, p.387.

10 Alexandra Richie, *Faust's Metropolis: A History of Berlin* (New York, 1998) p.406.

Chapter 6: 1933–1936 Old Surehand

1 Fest, *Hitler*, p.411.

2 Robert Gellately, *Backing Hitler* (New York, 2001) p.24.

3 Peter Gay, *My German Question: Growing Up in Nazi Berlin* (London, 1998) p.75.

4 Fest, *Hitler*, p.428.

5 Quoted in Gellately, *Backing Hitler*, p.260.

6 Diana Mosley to the author.

7 Gellately, *Backing Hitler*, p.259.

8 Toland, *Adolf Hitler*, p.501.

9 Fest, *Hitler*, p. 491.

10 Toland, *Adolf Hitler*, p.507.

11 *Ibid.*, p. 432.

12 *Ibid.*, p.407.

13 Fest, *Hitler*, p.451.

14 Quoted in Kershaw, *Hubris*, p.503.

15 Fest, *Hitler*, p.502.

16 Bullock, *Hitler*, p.379.

17 Toland, *Adolf Hitler*, p.699.

18 Fest, *Hitler*, p.479.

19 Toland, *Adolf Hitler*, p.536.

20 *Table Talk*, p.631.

21 Norman Stone, *Hitler* (London, 1980) p.55.

Chapter 7: 1936–1939 The Road to War

1 Toland, *Adolf Hitler*, p.644.

2 Hugh Trevor-Roper, *Last Days of Hitler*, p.66.

3 Fest, *Hitler*, p.511.

4 Richard J. Evans, *The Third Reich in Power* (London, 2003) p.582.

5 *Ibid.*, p.591.

6 *Ibid.*, p.604.

7 Toland, *Adolf Hitler*, p.736.

8 Stone, *Hitler*, p.73.

9 Quoted in Toland, *Adolf Hitler*, p.651.

10 C. V. Wedgwood, *The Last of the Radicals* (London, 1951) p.231.

11 Toland, *Adolf Hitler*, p.682.

12 *Ibid.*, p.559.

13 Brigitte Hamann, *Hitlers Wien* (Munich, 2000) p.306.

Chapter 8: 1939–1941 War Lord

1 Andrew Roberts, *The Storm of War* (London, 2009) p.39.

2 *Table Talk*, p.438.

3 Fest, *Hitler*, p.692.

4 Robert Wright, *Dowding and the Battle of Britain* (London, Macdonald & Co.) p.104.

5 Roberts, *Storm of War*, p.141.

6 Toland, *Adolf Hitler*, p.909.

7 *Table Talk*, p.583.

8 Reck-Malleczewen, *Diary of a Man in Despair*, p.124.

9 Toland, *Adolf Hitler*, p.910.

10 *Ibid.*, p 919.

11 *Table Talk*, p.8.

12 Toland, *Adolf Hitler*, p.977.

Chapter 9: The Final Solution

1 Hitler, *Mein Kampf*, p.49.

2 *Ibid.*, p.295.

3 *Table Talk*, p.314.

4 Quoted in Michael Burleigh, *The Third Reich: A New History* (London, 2001), p.660.

5 *Ibid.*

6 *Table Talk* p.618.

Chapter 10: 1941–1945 Defeat

1 Trevor-Roper, *The Last Days of Hitler*, p.68.

2 Fest, *Hitler*, p.710.

3 *Ibid.*, p.712.

4 Toland, *Adolf Hitler*, p.1117.

Chapter 11: The Bunker

1 *Table Talk*, p.81.

2 Richie, *Faust's Metropolis*, p.534.

3 Stone, *Hitler*, p.156.

4 *Table Talk*, p.135.

5 Richie, *Faust's Metropolis*, p.540.

6 *Table Talk*, p.206.

7 Burleigh, *The Third Reich*, p.591.

Chapter 12: Final Verdict

1 Thomas Carlyle, *Heroes and Hero-Worship*, Lecture VI.

2 Trevor-Roper, *Last Days of Hitler*, p.35.

3 *Ibid.*, p.44.

4 *Table Talk*, p.323.

5 *Ibid.*, p.322.

SELECT BIBLIOGRAPHY

Beevor, Antony, *Berlin: The Downfall, 1945*, London, Viking, 2004

Bullock, Alan, *Hitler: A Study in Tyranny*, New York, Harper, 1952

Burleigh, Michael, *The Third Reich, A New History*, London, Macmillan, 2001

Carlyle, Thomas, *Heroes, Hero-Worship and the Heroic in History*, New York, Charles Scribner (Complete Works of Thomas Carlyle), 1903

Clark, Alan, *Barbarossa*, London, Weidenfeld and Nicolson, 1995

Evans, Richard J., *The Third Reich in Power*, London, Allen Lane, 2003

Fest, Joachim, *Hitler*, London (English translation of work first published in Frankfurt – Ullstein, Germany, 1973), Weidenfeld & Nicolson, 1974

Gay, Peter, *My German Question. Growing Up in Nazi Berlin*, New Haven/London, Yale University Press, 1998

Gellately, Robert, *Backing Hitler*, New York/Oxford, Oxford University Press, 2001

Gellately, Robert, *The Gestapo and German Society*, New York/Oxford, Oxford University Press, 1990

Gerhard, Engel, *At the Heart of the Reich: the Secret Diary of Hitler's Army Adjutant Major Gerhard*. Notes and Introduction by Hildegard von Kotze; preface by Charles Messenger, translated by Geoffrey Brooks, London, Greenhill Books, 2005

Goebbels, Josef, *Tagebücher 1945. Die letzten Aufzeichnungen*, Hamburg, 1977

Hamann, Brigitte, *Hitlers Wien*, München, Piper Verlag, 2000

Hamann, Brigitte, *Winifred Wagner, oder Hitlers Bayreuth*, München, Piper Verlag, 2002

Hanfstaengl, Ernst, *Hitler: The Missing Years*, London, Eyre and Spottiswoode, 1958

Hauser, Heinrich, *Hitler Versus Germany*, London, Jarrolds, 1940

Hitler, Adolf, *Mein Kampf*, München, Zentralverlag der NSDAP, 1938

Hitler's Table Talk 1941–1944, Introduced with a new Preface by Hugh Trevor-Roper, New York, Enigma Books (translated by Norman Cameron and R. H. Stevens), 1953

Kershaw, Ian, *Hitler, 1889–1936: Hubris*, London, Allen Lane, Penguin, 1998

Kershaw, Ian, *Hitler, 1936–1945: Nemesis*, Allen Lane, Penguin, 2000

Kubizek, August, *Young Hitler, The Story of Our Friendship*, London, Allan Wingate, 1954

Maser, Werner, *Hitler, Legend, Myth and Reality*, New York, Harper & Row Publishers, 1973

Overy, Richard, *The Dictators: Hitler's Germany and Stalin's Russia*, London, Allen Lane, 2004

Reck-Malleczewen, Friedrich Percyval, *Diary of a Man in Despair*, London, Audiogrove Ltd (first published in Germany as *Tagebuch eines Verzweifelten*, 1947), 1997

Richie, Alexandra, *Faust's Metropolis, A History of Berlin*, New York, Carroll & Graf, 1998

Roberts, Andrew, *Hitler and Churchill, Secrets of Leadership*, London, Weidenfeld and Nicolson, 2003

Roberts, Andrew, *The Holy Fox. A Biography of Lord Halifax*, London, Weidenfeld and Nicolson, 1991

Roberts, Andrew, *The Storm of War*, London, Allen Lane, 2009

Speer, Albert, *Inside the Third Reich*, London, Weidenfeld and Nicolson, 1970

Spotts, Frederic, *Hitler and the Power of Aesthetics*, London, Hutchinson, 2002

Steinert, Marlis, *Hitler*, Paris, Librairie Arthème Fayard, 1991

Steinert, Marlis, *Hitlers Krieg und die Deutschen. Stimmung und Haltung der Deutschen Bevölkerung im Zweiten Weltkrieg*, Düsseldorf/Vienna, 1970

Stone, Norman, *Hitler*, London, Hodder and Stoughton, 1980

Toland, John, *Adolf Hitler*, New York, Doubleday and Co., 1976

Trevor-Roper, Hugh, *The Last Days of Hitler*, London, Macmillan & Co. Ltd, 1947

Wagner, Friedelind, *The Royal Family of Bayreuth*, London, Eyre and Spottiswoode, 1948

Weber, Thomas, *Hitler's first war: Adolf Hitler, the man of the List regiment, and the First World War*, Oxford, Oxford University Press, 2010

Wedgwood, C.V, *The Last of the Radicals*, London, Jonathan Cape, 1951

Wright, Robert, *Dowding and the Battle of Britain*, London, Macdonald & Co., 1969

Zitelmann, Rainer, *Hitler, Selbstverständnis eines Revolutionärs*, Hamburg/Leamington Spa/New York, Berg, 1987

INDEX

Index

Fuchs, Marta, 128
Führer (Leader), 8, 36, 78, 189

Galland, Adolf, 138
Gas attack, 20
Gassing of Jews, 154, 155
Gauleiters, 55, 77, 107, 108, 175
Gay, Peter, 88
Gdansk, 125
Gellately, Robert, 90–91
George, David Lloyd, 10
German army
    fear of Communism in, 24, 25–26
    fear of Left in, 76
    Hitler and, 94, 96, 97–98
    Rommel and, 158–159
German exiles, 150
German nationalism, 76
Hitler family and, 14
German people
disillusionment with Hitler, 163
    failure to recognize true nature
        of Hitler and Nazis, 85–87,
        89–90, 106
    relief when Nazis came to power,
        89–91
    resilient response to war, 172–173
    response to invasion of Poland
        and start of war, 127–128
    support for Hitler, 89–91, 126–127
German Right
    fear of Communism, 79
    on German defeat in First World
        War, 24–25
    splinter parties of, 29

German Workers Party, 29
Germany
    attempted putsch in, 43–46
    defeat in First World War, 7–8,
        21–22
    economic crisis in, 7–8, 37–38, 65
    economic recovery under Nazis,
        10, 98, 106, 109
    fractured government following
        stock market crash, 67–68, 77,
        79–83
    Jewish persecution effect on
        economy, 152–153
    negotiation over reparations, 37
    resistance movement in, 161–164
    See also Weimar Republic
Gestapo (Geheime Staatsolizei), 85
Giesler, Hermann, 135
Goebbels, Helga, 179
Goebbels, Joseph, 35, 94, 173
    in Berlin bunker, 177, 179
    Hitler and, 53–55, 70
    Hitler's rise to Chancellorship and,
        78, 79, 81
    Nuremberg rally and, 63, 64
    Roman Catholicism and, 71
    violence against Jews and, 115,
        141
Goebbels, Magda, 179
Gombrich, Ernst, 150
Göring, Hermann, 39, 91, 94, 97,
    141
    assassination attempt against
        Hitler and, 165, 166
    attempted putsch and, 41, 43

205

Index

assumption of presidency, 97
attempted putsch and, 41–43
audience for, 35–36
as author of Final Solution, 154, 156
Battle of the Bulge and, 168–169
belief in modernity, 186–187
in Berlin bunker, 171–172, 175–179
bombing of British cities and, 137–138
childhood, 4–5, 12, 14–15
citizenship of, 8
clique surrounding, 38–39, 52–54, 56–58
coalition governments and, 68
as Commander in Chief, 98
consolidation of Nazi party under, 55–56
cult of personality, 31–32
dismantling of Czechoslovakia and, 124
dogs and, 18–19, 20, 61, 70, 168, 173–174, 177, 179
domestic life of, 62–63, 69–70
as draft-dodger, 8–9, 16
Eva Braun and, 112–113, 173, 174, 176, 178, 179
extraordinariness of, 188–189
female patrons, 56–58
German army and, 94, 96, 97–98
on German overpopulation, 153
goal of Second World War and, 131–132
Hess's flight to Scotland and, 140–141

hypochondria of, 14, 62, 111–112
indolence of, 5–7, 95
on inevitability of war, 118–119
invasion of Soviet Union and, 132, 142, 143
Japan and, 145–147
lack of leadership skills/qualities, 20, 188
lack of skills, 9–10
as magician, 27, 76, 127, 189–190
as mass-murderer, 1–2
May Day march, 39
mental health of, 109, 110–111, 176
military service of, 9, 16–21
Mitford and, 103–105
National Socialist rally of 1920, 31–33
Night of the Long Knives and, 96–97
Obersalzberg (Berghof) and, 60–61, 62–63
opera and, 15, 32–33, 35
oratorical skills, 24, 26–30, 188–189
ordinariness of beliefs, 1–4, 184–188
physical health of, 113–114, 160–161
plans for expansion, 107–110
political manipulation skills of, 30
political negotiation ability of, 33–34
politics of mass emotion and, 28–29

207

Hitler (*continued*)
  in prison, 46–49
  program for Germany, 47–48
  public rallies and, 31–33, 55–56,
    63–64, 71, 80, 98–99
  as reader, 11
  reasons for rise to power, 183–190
  relationship with niece Geli,
    62–63, 68–69, 70
  religion and, 71–73, 185–186
  on resilience of German people,
    173
  response to fire in Reichstag, 93
  rise to power, 23–24, 70, 79,
    81–83
  Roman Catholicism and, 71–73
  Rothermere and, 91
  as savior to German people, 8
  sexuality of, 61–62
  socioeconomic background of,
    4–5, 12
  spoken word and, 27–28
  success of economic program, 10,
    90–91, 106, 109
  suicide of, 1, 179
  surrender of French and, 134, 135
  sycophancy of, 57
  Table Talk, 144–145, 186
  trial of for putsch attempt, 43–46
  unemployment of, 4–6
  use of tantrums, 9–10, 110, 120
  visit to Paris, 135–136
  Wagner and, 5, 11, 15, 31, 45,
    181–182
  war with U.S. and, 158

  as youth in Vienna, 15–16
  *See also Mein Kampf (My
    Struggle)* (Hitler)
Hitler, Alois, 5, 12–13
Hitler, Angela, 13
Hitler, Edmund, 14
Hitler, Gustav, 13
Hitler, Ida, 14
Hitler, Johanna, 14
Hitler, Klara Pölzl, 5, 13, 14, 16,
    111–112, 121
Hitler, Otto, 14
Hitler, Paula, 14
Hitler, William Patrick, 13
Hitler Youth (Hitler Jugend), 74–75,
    80
HJ. *See* Hitler Youth (Hitler Jugend)
Hoffmann, Heinrich, 112–113
Hope, offered by Hitler, 36
Horoscopes, 140–141
Housing shortage, confiscation of
    Jewish property and, 153–154
Human Comedy (Balzac), 3
Hume, David, 181
Hungary
  pro-Nazi population in, 139
  removal of Jews in, 155
Huntziger, Charles, 134

In the Land of the Mahdi (May), 11
Iron Cross, 18
Irrationality of crowds, 189–190
"I Say Yes!" (Hauptmann), 89
Italy, Pact of Steel, 126. *See also*
    Mussolini, Benito

208

Index